A HISTORY
OF THE
WORLD IN
50 PIECES

A HISTORY OF THE WORLD IN 50 PIECES

THE CLASSICAL MUSIC THAT SHAPES US

TOM SERVICE

BBC
BOOKS

BBC BOOKS

UK | USA | Canada | Ireland | Australia
India | New Zealand | South Africa

BBC Books is part of the Penguin Random House group of companies
whose addresses can be found at global.penguinrandomhouse.com

Penguin Random House UK
One Embassy Gardens, 8 Viaduct Gardens, London SW11 7BW

penguin.co.uk
global.penguinrandomhouse.com

Penguin
Random House
UK

First published by BBC Books in 2025
1

Typeset by seagulls.net

Printed and bound in Great Britain by Clays Ltd, Elcograf S.p.A.

The authorised representative in the EEA is Penguin Random House Ireland,
Morrison Chambers, 32 Nassau Street, Dublin D02 YH68.

A CIP catalogue record for this book is available from the British Library

ISBN 9781785949371

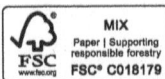

For GMS and JMS.

CONTENTS

INTRODUCTION

A History of the World in 50 Pieces – a title from which a few questions naturally flow: whose history? whose world? whose pieces? Part of the answer, if you review the list of chapters ahead of you in this miscellany, which traces its fragmentary history through some of the music that we have made as human beings, might easily be: for all its attempts to circumnavigate global music across time, history, geography, and culture, this is a Northern-hemisphere-biased, temporally-unbalanced, myopically Western, metro-centric, 'classical'-heavy selection that no one else on the planet apart from this writer would have come up with.

And that's true. So, what is this collection, and what is it trying to achieve, in the context of all of those limitations?

This isn't a history of music. Instead it's a constellation-like history of how music shapes, and has been shaped by, the contours of what it means to be human. It's a story revealed through the choice of a 50-part collection of pieces, each opening a window on the times and places of their creation, but resonating further and wider with other currents of social change, politics and culture.

It's a world that's created through the connections across time and place of the pieces I've chosen so that, arranged chronologically, a composite picture emerges of how the dance between music and our species has produced some of the most powerful expressions of what it means to be human over the last few millennia, and even further back in time.

The crucial idea is what a 'piece' of music or classical music actually is. It's my definition of that idea that's guided the field of choice, from what would otherwise be a near infinity of possibility. So, in those terms, what is a 'piece of music'? It's something whose transmission, either in oral cultures, through the handing on of embodied tradition, or through symbolic representation as written notation, allows music both to be part of the time and place of its creation and to be independent of it. Whatever the means of their ongoing communication, pieces of music are performative practices that can be endlessly reinterpreted by communities and cultures of performers and listeners. They are musical phenomena that belong to whoever sings them, plays them, and hears them, at whatever distance of time and place to the circumstances of their creation.

This is the democratic principle of a 'piece of music': through whatever means they are passed on from place to place, from culture to culture, from voice to voice, and player to player, pieces of music function as musical promises that are redeemed and claimed in the future by persons and cultures unknown to their original creators. This is a magical process through time and across geography, in which future music-makers and listeners receive these pieces of music as if they were meant for them, to be remade by them, to become theirs. Transcending time, these pieces are both inexorably tied to the context of their creation – and fly free of it.

That definition means there are things that a 'piece of music' isn't: this isn't a compendium of 50 events that have been significant for musical history, and it's not a list of favourite recordings of songs or symphonies. The reason for this is that one-off events and fixed-in-time recordings would create a pantheon of musical and historical greatest hits, and that's not the point of this book. It's not only about songs that have been sung, performances that have happened, fixed in the aspic of a musical museum. Instead, this book is a cornucopia of music-making that hasn't yet happened, as much as music that has.

The pieces of music in this book thrum and teem with the potential of the musicking that they will continue to inspire in the future, in the way they're taken up by musical communities we don't know yet: this music belongs to them, just as much as it belongs to us.

So what has guided the selection of the 50 pieces, and the 50 chapters? The broad ideas were not to reflect a judgement that these pieces are 'better' than the billions of others out there, and not to make a hierarchy of musical quality or qualities – ineluctably contested terms, contingent on who's making the assessment, where, and when, at every stage of human history. Instead, the pieces make up a chronological sequence of music to attend to, in the biggest sense. To listen to, of course, but also to pay attention to the individual, social, political, and so many other contexts they reflect.

The self-imposed definition of 'pieces of music' that I've just outlined is occasionally expanded beyond those limits.

That's most obviously true in the Prologue, the pre-piece era, and the songs of the humpback whale, in which we encounter the sounds of the natural world and the cosmos. The reason they're there is that our human-made music is a subset of the songs that the Earth and the planets sing. Our interpretation of these sounds turns them into pieces of human perception that reveal other dimensions of the musical connections that bind us not only to each other but to the vibrating frequencies and energies of all matter in the universe: the piece of music of which we are all an infinitesimal part.

Yet we are an important and a joyous part of that panoply. Over millennia, our music-making has sounded the ecstatic communion of our coming together in social groups, around fires, in caves, in concert halls. Music is the sound of our love and our faith, it's the resonance of our connection with each other, it's a song that keeps singing across the generations in how these 50 pieces belong to us, and to our future.

And as well as the connections you might feel, from Enheduanna to Pauline Oliveros, from Hildegard of Bingen to Kaija Saariaho, there are countless gaps you will experience in the 50 chapters, as we move from Songlines to symphonies, from operas to sounds inspired by the ocean. That's where your listening and imagination comes in: just as the pieces themselves are messages to be reinterpreted, to become things unknowable by their creators, so too is this 50-part collection an invitation to make your own journeys in your listening and music-making, to keep exploring what it means to be musical – which is the same as saying: what it means to be human.

PROLOGUE: THE PRE-PIECE ERA

The rotation of the Earth – the Laetoli footprints
– the earliest instruments – the Songlines

It's literally beneath us: under every step we take, below the range of our hearing, imperceptible unless recorded by the magic of microphones that have the sensitivity to pick it up – the sound of the rotation of the Earth.

And there *is* a recording of this primordial sound: on the composer and sound recordist Jez riley French's *in limitless geologies*, an album that came out in 2023 after he'd been working on it for a decade, that's what you can hear. Or rather, that's what you feel in your solar plexus as well as perceive with your ears: the sounds of the world turning are felt as a full-body immersion, since their frequencies extend down into the realms of the infrasonic, below the threshold of our hearing, but sensed by our bodies as vibrations. You feel the pressure waves pulsing through the air on your skin; you feel your cells being shaken by these low, deep swells. When you're experiencing the sounds of the

Earth's rotation, they are physically churning the viscera of your body.

It's a sound found by microphones going where human beings cannot, inside geothermal vents and fumaroles in Iceland. Between the tectonic plates of Eurasia and North America, the Earth's skin is broken in Iceland. Jez riley French used specially designed contact microphones, placed directly on surfaces to allow us to perceive their reverberation, and geo-phones that were originally designed for oil exploration, which are turned into listening sensors for the deep under-ground. Plunged inside these geological wounds, they pick up the sounds of the Earth's eastward rotation, magnetic energy transformed into sonic material.

This is the true song of the Earth: the piece that our planet has been performing for the last four and a half billion years, the sound of the living Earth. As well as the wonder of feeling these soundwaves course through your body, they are sublime, uncanny, even terrifying. They are definitely not comforting or cosseting: instead they're a stomach-sinking abyss that feels like a confrontation between human time set against the deep-est time of the spinning Earth's life-span.

Yet, like our bodies, these sounds are alive and ever-chang-ing. The rotation of the Earth's song isn't a constant underscore, but a shifting current of energy, as the Earth's rotational axis tilts, as its speed of rotation changes, so that no day is exactly the same length as the next – our days are milliseconds longer than they were centuries ago.

Listening to these sounds from deep inside the Earth is a revelation of the cosmic essentials without which no life on Earth could survive: without its rotation, without its tides, without its planetary dance through space. But it's also a reminder that the music of the spheres of the solar system, of deep space, and the whole universe, are spectacularly indifferent to the timescales of our lives. They are galactic musical scores in which our lives are an infinitesimal yet interconnected part. They make the fundamental piece of music on which our lives dance, mayflies on a deep river of time.

Yet we are here: and our own bodies are constellations of frequencies of vibration, the rhythms of our limbs, our pulses, our cells and systems coursing in syncopation, and harmony, and friction; and they are the result of the other long-term dance of which we are merely the latest iteration: evolution, another of nature's underscores upon which our lives are lived.

And to find traces of the rhythms that our hominid ancestors moved to, there is amazing evidence that was discovered in Tanzania in 1976: three sets of footprints, preserved in ancient lava-flows at Laetoli. Dating from around 3.7 million years ago, these are the footprints of three of our bipedal ancestors, Australopithecus afarensis, and we can follow them for 27 metres over 70 impressions in the ash before they disappear. They are as well preserved as if they had walked on a sandy beach yesterday; the aeons shrink breathtakingly when you look at them and imagine the relationships between these three individuals: were they members of the same community, tribe, or family group?

The Laetoli footprints are the earliest tracks yet discovered of our hominid ancestors. But they are also the first proto-human musical score. The musical notation of today's musical cultures fixes time into place with printed notes on the page. And that's what these footprints do too. They fix and record the time of these three Australopithecines in the landscape, 3.7 million years ago. The imprints of their feet are the first impressions of the regular pulsation of human-ancestral bodies on the earth – the first fragment of hominid-made rhythmic notation in world history.

They are physically close to each other, so much so that one set of prints follows in the track of another; they are walking with a relaxed stroll, crossing what was likely a more forested landscape in their time than the environment of today's Rift Valley. These three – either a female, a male, and a child, or two males and a female, research suggests – are caught and captured in a moment of transcendent mundanity in the middle of their lives.

In his book *Sound Tracks*, the archaeologist Graeme Lawson asks the question whether we might one day be able to interpret these tracks to detect 'changes in their sense of time, and timing, and rhythm: changes that would eventually take on modern symbolic meanings as music and dance?' Yet there is much that the Laetoli tracks already reveal: scientifically, these footprints are conclusive proof that our hominid ancestors developed the ability to walk on two legs before the modern human brain evolved, and the rhythms that they already disclose amount to a kind of music that we can all recognise: our walking, the polyphony of our limbs working in concert. Without yet being able to understand their precise relationships, we can imagine the communication their voices and bodies might have created: sounds of reassurance and community, their feet making a route over this terrain for the one and only time that we can be sure they took this path, on a journey, perhaps, towards bigger family groups, to find more fertile terrain, to gather food, to survive.

So these footprints aren't silent: all it takes is our imagination to put our contemporary Homo sapiens bodies in the place of our ancestors, to walk in their footsteps, to feel that corporeal connection over millions of years, across boundaries of species as well as time, through the sound and squelch of their feet in the ash and mud they walked through.

There can be no physical trace left of the vocal sounds that these ancestral bodies made. But the musical culture of our more recent ancestry, the Homo sapiens of tens of thousands of years ago, and the repertoires they might have made together, is within the grasp of our understanding.

In the cave system of Chauvet in the Ardèche in France, the cave paintings, made over 30,000 years ago, are shocking in their immediacy, vibrancy, skill – and their preservation. Acoustic research at Chauvet, and in other sites of cave paintings all over the world, demonstrates that where the cave art is most dense and elaborate, the resonance of the space is richest. That suggests that these were places that were chosen because of how they sounded, the way that voices echo the most powerfully and the most uncannily, not merely because painted marks would stick to the walls. And if this acoustic phenomenon was recognised and important to the community, it might have made them places of special significance for celebration, for ritual, or even for communion with otherworldly presences, sounded in the spectral echoing of their voices.

Did they mark the times of their lives, celebrate hunts, and hear mysterious reverberations of their voices in caves like these? Were they using their voices to conjure the spiritual implications of hearing their voices returning to them as if from another world? The material evidence of the paintings is staggering, but the connection with sound-making, dancing, musicking bodies is even more spine-tingling.

And while the sounds made by the voices of early European Homo sapiens have disappeared into the echoing spaces of caves in France, Germany and Spain, we do have incontrovertible evidence of other sounds that these societies produced – in the instruments they made. At the Geißenklösterle cave in south-west Germany, bone flutes have been discovered, dating from 42–43,000 years ago. Although distant in time from us, it is still many millennia after our 300,000-year-old species first arrived in Eurasia from Africa. The bone flutes are made from the wing-bones of a vulture and a mammoth bone, and in recreations made by archaeologist Wulf Hein, it's possible to hear the music that the bird-bone flute can make.

The flute produces sounds whose power pierces through the millennia: the technology and understanding required to produce this instrument must have built on previous generations of skills, and countless other flutes made before this example. Its five finger holes make a striking link with the pentatonic, or five-note scales that so many folk melodies all over the world are still made from, a window into the repertoire of pieces and songs this flute could have inspired and accompanied. The high register and soundworld of this instrument also makes it uniquely capable of mimicking birdsong, reproducing the sounds of the animal that gave its life to make it.

The need to make music, like the need to make cave paintings, demonstrates how the earliest European humans were engaged in remaking and rethinking their world through cultures that were about much more than survival. They were capable of symbolic representation of the world around them, conceiving and re-conceiving their lives in ways that our modern musical cultures continue, and to which they are connected.

And where there were flutes, there was also clearly much more that we haven't yet found. The Geißenklösterle flutes are only exceptional because of their discovery: they are among the earliest that we modern humans have found, but they are far from the first instruments ever made. Not least because, in the Divje Babe cave in Slovenia, a carved bear femur has been claimed as evidence of Neanderthal music instrument manufacture, dating from 50–60,000 years BC.

Another human-made flute fragment from 110,000 years ago, a single hole carved in a tiny curve of bone, from the Haua Fteah cave in Libya, is currently the oldest constructed evidence of instrument-making we have, showing just how early in the history of Homo sapiens instrumental music developed – and that fragment itself is only a tiny piece of the iceberg of our human musicking.

And yet it's not only in artefacts – we don't have to look through archaeological digs. We can listen to song-makers in Australia to hear the most ancient continuous tradition of song-making on our planet: the Songlines of the First Peoples of Australia. With a history stretching back 65,000 years, there are records in these songs of events that are confirmed by archaeology and geology, shifts of climate and territory and terrain, as well as the trauma of the recent history of Australia's colonisation. The vast repertoire of Songlines are a living record of those networked pasts and presents, and they are among the most precious, most complex, and most awe-inspiring phenomena that human minds and bodies have ever created. Held as an ongoing oral tradition, Songlines are simultaneously a repertoire, a means of map-making and way-faring, a living history of myth, metaphor and physical reality, and a chart of the interconnectedness of the human, the animal, the landscape and the cosmos.

The Songlines' sheer physics are enough to blow the minds of any modern human: especially Western-influenced minds for whom knowledge, instead of a corporeal resource of feeling and being, is a commodity to be bought and sold, and for whom the ideology of technological progress means our digital maps and our digitally-produced songs in our present tense must be the most efficient, the most useful, the most complete.

That's a delusion. The Songlines are arguably the most sophisticated system of embodied knowledge ever developed, and they come not from technology but from the ancestors, and from the earth. Practically speaking, Songlines are, in part, about navigation, enabling travel from one side of the continent of Australia to the other. If you know the songs, you can journey safely from the east to the west of Australia, thanks to the symbiotic relationship between the songs and the land. The land is sung into being, and the song harbours the future of your journey through the landmarks you see, the rivers you cross, the animals who share the landscape with you, the collective history of your ancestors' relationship with these places. The Seven Sisters Songline – a creation myth based on the Pleiades constellation – crosses the entire continent, a Songline that individual communities have responsibility for preserving, for singing the part of the story that relates to their place and their own history, their chain in a 2,500-mile-long piece of collective memory and music. The Seven Sisters Songline is arguably the longest, grandest and most significant piece of human-made music, storytelling and cultural knowledge that's ever been created. Other Songlines are made for particular people and specific locations, with information on where water and food can be found and harvested. Sung by single voices, and in community, with repeated melodic figures and rhythmic patterns, sometimes using sticks on the ground as percussion, the landscape and the history of a continent can be sung into being.

Yet the Songlines aren't a fixed repertoire, an absolute order of words and sounds that simply needs to be learnt by rote and handed down through the generations – epic enough as even that idea is. The store of memory that the Songlines contain and reflect is astounding, but still more remarkable is the ever-changing quality of the songs, how they are sung, and who sings them. That has meant a period of horrifying fragility in their recent history, when the colonisation of Australia initiated policies of cultural extermination, which could have cleared the world of its Songlines. Yet the collective memory across fractured and ravaged communities of indigenous peoples persisted, and the Songlines today are – at last – celebrated, and appreciated, their unique contribution to human history recognised.

The Songlines reveal the truth that a place – any place – is multi-dimensional in time, space, memory and meaning, and they are the most complete way that human cultures have ever developed of singing those deep relationships into being. The Songlines principle is transformative because it's relational: their performance enacts a relationship with place, with the past, with the interdependence of all living things, in which the singer in the present tense is simply another dot in time, one point among an infinite number that coalesce and collide with one another, arcing back to the aeons of the first singers of the Songlines – who, in indigenous wisdom, emerge at the same time as the Earth, being indivisible from it, as we all are.

Communities handing tradition on in a never-ending chain of musical present-tenses through each generation: all musical cultures are, at least in part, oral traditions, and all are the work of the collective effort of whole populations. Who came up with the first Songline? Gods, animals, the earth itself: human individuals are less important than the communal ownership of the Songlines, in their performance, preservation and transformation.

Even if we are not all privileged to be singers of Songlines in Australia, we are all connected by the same principle, singing and sharing the Songlines of our own lives, the courses they run in space and time, in sound and song – and in the 50 pieces that follow in this book.

PIECE #1

ENHEDUANNA

HYMNS

Ur, Mesopotamia, c. 2300 BC

Continents to the west, leaping across centuries, we find the first creative work in the human imagination that has a single named author.

She is Enheduanna, high priestess of the city of Ur in Mesopotamia, present-day Iraq. 45 of her poems survive on cuneiform tablets, mostly written for separate temples in the Akkadian Empire. These lyrics were designed to be performed as part of a thriving musical, spiritual and ritual culture as contemporary iconography and evidence shows. These poems were hymns performed in honour of the moon deity she worshipped, Nanna, in the twenty-fourth century BC.

Enheduanna's lineage was aristocratic. She was a princess, the daughter of the Emperor Sargon the Great, and part of a society in Mesopotamia that can claim the first literary language, and the first modern empire. The politics were part of the poetry and the songs. Enheduanna's lyrics are designed to fuse together the cults of the primary deities of the northern and southern regions of Mesopotamia that Sargon ruled over, Ishtar and Inanna.

Enheduanna belonged to a culture of striking equality of the sexes in all aspects of society, from work to property rights to visibility in religious ritual, and the poems attributed to her put images of female power front and centre in their storytelling. In one of the poems, Inanna fights Ebih, a personification of an entire mountain range. She makes the landscape collapse, and in the final encounter with Ebih, Enheduanna's poem reads: Inanna 'sharpened both edges of her dagger. She grabbed Ebih's neck as if ripping up esparto grass. She pressed the dagger's teeth into its interior. She roared like thunder. The rocks forming the body of Ebih clattered down its flanks.'

Not only war-like, the songs are also paeans of praise for the Mesopotamian landscape, and, above all, for the process of composing these lyrics. 'The Exaltation of Inanna' is a raw and devastating poem to her Goddess that was written in human terror and divine faith after Enheduanna had been forced out of the city of Ur: 'I am dying / that I must sing / this sacred song'. In it, she also claims and celebrates her authorial role: 'I have given birth / Oh exalted lady, (to this song) for you / That which I recited to you at (mid)night / May the singer repeat it to you at noon!'

The question is what that singer would have sounded like, and what instruments they might have played. We know that Mesopotamian musical culture before the time of Enheduanna included flutes, played by women, as well as harps, drums and other wind instruments. A lamentation prayer from around 2000 BC bewails the destruction of Sumer's cities, and the end of 'sweet-sounding musical instruments such as the lyre, drum, tambourine, and reed pipe; no comforting songs and soothing words from the temple singers and priests'. Other depictions of religious music-making show female musicians playing the balaĝ, a lyre-like instrument, which was associated with the goddess Ninigizibara.

Enheduanna's songs were copied dozens of times after her lifetime; the structure and expression of her temple hymns were a vital influence for centuries on future composers and writers. The texts survive, but the sounds that would have accompanied these songs in temples and across Mesopotamian culture need to be reimagined from the representation of musical instruments and religious performance on reliefs and the images carved on cylinder seals.

Yet Enheduanna's legacy lives on, in the work of every composer, author and artist who has signed their own work for the last four and a half millennia. At the end of her last temple hymn, Enheduanna reveals herself, and claims her work as her own: 'the person who bound this tablet together is Enheduanna / my king / something never before created / did not this one give birth to it'. And in those words, she jumps across the aeons to speak to every creative artist who has lived and worked and claimed their compositions in word and music as their own.

PIECE #2

THE ORESTES FRAGMENT

Greece, c. 200 BC

The iconography of Ancient Greek music and its enormous instrumentarium, like the aulos – a double-pipe instrument, played with one pipe in each hand – the lyres, the cytharas, the drums and percussion, in celebration, in ritual, and in daily life, seems like a musical treasure trove. But finding evidence for what they actually sounded like, and the music they actually played and which their voices sang, has proved speculative at best, and a fool's errand at worst. In 1932, Wilfrid Perrett reported the scholarly view that: 'Nobody has ever made head or tail of ancient Greek music, and nobody ever will. That way madness lies'.

But the twenty-first century has found revelation where previous generations thought there could only be silence and confusion. That's thanks to research led by Armand D'Angour, who has worked on the fragments of musical notation that survived from a period in history in which no written evidence is usually thought to be translatable into sound. Not true: there are around 60 fragments from Ancient Greece that show indications not only of rhythm and pitch, but melody and expression.

And D'Angour's essential point is that everything we call poetry in the Ancient World, from Homer to Sappho, was made – composed – as a text to be sung, and to be performed with instrumental accompaniment. The rhythmic feet of Greek poetry is a meter not only of words, but of sound and rhythm: the hexameter, the six-beat pattern of Homer's *Iliad*, is already a proto-music, a swing of accents strong and soft, a pattern of rhyme that suggests its own speech melody.

But mere speech wouldn't have been enough for Homer or for any of the Greek poets or writers. They weren't only composers of texts, but creators and inspirers of music. The musicologist Stefan Hagel has reconstructed the four-note lyre that Homer used, and his improvised performances of the *Iliad* are a window into what these texts were meant to sound like. To hear them only as words would have been to experience only part of their meaning and expression. D'Angour's research, and the work of virtuosic musicologists, instrument-builders and performers, gives us a viscerally noisy sense of what we have all been missing in our understanding of Ancient Greek culture.

And when you hear a performance of the most important fragment of notation that survives – a passage from Euripides' *Orestes*, originally written in 408 BC, in which the chorus describe Orestes being chased by the Furies conjured by his mother, Clytemnestra, whom he has murdered – the Ancient world jumps thrillingly into our time. This moment from Euripides' ancient tragedy, preserved on a torn fragment of papyrus from around 200 BC, just a couple of inches square, becomes a contemporary soundscape.

Thanks to the virtuosity of Barnaby Brown, playing the aulos, in the first performances of this piece since the fifth century BC, in Oxford in 2017, the voices of the chorus are quickened by a repeated phrase on the pipes that's perfectly descriptive of this terrifying hunt, and impossible to get out of your head when you've heard it. The *Orestes* fragment is a piece that opens up a whole world in just a couple of minutes: centuries of research leading up to the moment of its performance, showing everyone that what was thought to be a culture defined by text was, in fact, teeming with music.

The whole concept of musical notation, the specificity of mark-making to record melody, rhythm and pitch, doesn't begin in the European world in the ninth century, as it's often thought to, but right here in Ancient Greece. The *Orestes* fragment is among the first, and the most inspirational, pieces of music in the Western imagination. It's a text for music, part of a multi-dimensional theatrical experience: in other words, it's a crucible of the phenomenon we now call opera – and that's a story we'll pick up in a couple of millennia's time …

PIECE #3
MALKAUNS RAGA

India, before 1000 AD

This is a raga composed, according to Hindu legend, by a goddess: the roots of the Malkauns raga lie in a story in which Parvati succeeds in seducing Lord Shiva, calming him from his vengeful killing spree after the death of his wife, Sati. Shiva doesn't know that Vishnu, the Preserver, reincarnated Sati as Parvati; it's her singing of the Malkauns raga that comforts Shiva, and brings his trail of destruction to an end. Basking in the halo of the power of the Malkauns raga, Shiva and Parvati are married, and Shiva is inspired to resurrect everyone he has murdered. The Malkauns raga's origin story is a parable of music's supernatural healing power.

In Indian tradition, ragas as ancient as Malkauns aren't composed by human beings but instead discovered by them as musical and spiritual phenomena, as gifts from the gods and goddesses. Malkauns, as one of the oldest surviving ragas, discovered in the first millennium BC, is imbued with special significance in the hands of its performers across the traditions of Indian music. Malkauns is renowned for its ability to relieve anxiety in human listeners as well as its divine audiences, and has a special power to cure headaches and stomach pains. It was even used in an experiment with a listenership of cows, to see how they would react to the musical balm of Malkauns. They didn't produce more milk, but did become more energetic.

Yet for its performers, Malkauns needs to be handled with care – and not only with respect to the time of day of its performance: Malkauns is associated with the small hours of the morning, from midnight until 3 a.m. Under the surface of its pentatonic melodic architecture, the great improvisers of Indian classical music know that they're dealing with spiritual material that has dangerous as well as healing potential. In the wrong hands, Malkauns can release the very demons that Parvati managed to calm in Shiva. As the sarod virtuoso Ustad Ali Akbar Khan said: 'If you're not in a serious mood, then don't play or sing Malkauns ... It is a favourite raga of the djinns ... If you can charm them – if they like the way you are playing it – they will do anything for you. If they don't – they will kill you.'

And Malkauns's special reputation is inherent not only in its origin myths and its spiritual reputation, but in its musical substance. Those five notes are a distinctive collection of pitches among the repertoire of the oldest ragas, and they contain worlds of ambiguity in how they can be interpreted, depending on the gravity that players give to each particular note of the scale, and how they shape the flow of their performances of Malkauns, which can last an hour or more. Malkauns can sound lamenting and joyful; it can be full of radiance or melancholy, depending on whether you're listening to the raga performed by the sarod of Abhisek Ladri or the vocals of Ustad Hamid Ali Khan, by the sitar-playing of Viram Jasani or the jazz trumpet of Don Cherry.

Producing all of that expressive complexity from the kernel of simplicity of those five notes: the Malkauns raga is a piece whose continual interpretation over the centuries is still conjuring sounds of divine comfort and vertiginously intoxicating intensity, as its musicians keep trying to keep the djinns on their side, and their audiences, like Lord Shiva, entranced.

PIECE #4

CANTILLATION

THE CHANTS OF JUDAISM AND THE OTHER ABRAHAMIC FAITHS

2500 BC onwards

Judaism is the oldest monotheistic religion, and has had a continuous tradition of chanting for the last 2,500 years that's as rich and diverse as its communities all over the world. The cantors, who lead the worship in synagogues with their voices, enact a symbiosis of word and melody and scriptural meaning in every service. And that means it's impossible to separate the Torah, the ur-piece of Judaism, from how it's sung, how it's performed and how it sounds in this cantillation tradition. The Masoretes, the scribe-scholars of Judaism, who worked in Palestine from the fifth century onwards, developed a system of accents, known as diacritics, written around the text, so that the inflections of the words can be clearly communicated. And this system also allows for personal interpretation in the different voices of the countless cantors in all the communities who have adopted this system, and who have chanted the texts ever since it became common practice, from the thirteenth century.

There is also the cheironomy that some cantors use, an equally rich system of hand-gestures that mimics the shape of the accents, so cantors lead their congregations physically as well as musically. It's a performance of the text in which not only the voice but the whole body is engaged in spiritual work. That's what the tradition of chanting the Hebrew Bible is all about, from every child coming of age in their bat- and bar-mitzvahs performing their first stretch of scripture in public to the most experienced female and male cantors, who are themselves building on a tradition that arcs back through the millennia, across all of the Jewish communities who have ever sung the fundamental piece of their faith.

And scripture and liturgy are sung, chanted and declaimed in all of the Abrahamic religions. The recitation traditions of the Koran reflect the musical and spiritual environments of the Middle East and Africa, with different scales used according to whether the preacher's background is in Cairo or Medina, in Senegal or Gambia – and reflecting the very earliest Islamic traditions in which the Koran was communicated as an oral tradition among Mohammed and his companions before it was written down.

Christian plainchant, developing from the older tradi-tions of Jewish cantillation, begins as a mnemonic practice in which scripture and liturgy were communicated in a pre-lit-erary world through the rise and fall of speech melodies. The chants transitioned from an oral tradition to a written reper-toire after the development of a formally developed system of notation in the Church around the ninth century, which also meant the possibility of named composers contributing chant compositions to the liturgy. That's a phenomenon that reaches fulfilment in composers like the ninth-century Abbess Kassiani in Constantinople, the first named female composer of chants, whose most celebrated and complex chant, the *Hymn of Kassia*, is still sung in the liturgy on Holy Wednesday.

All of these scriptural traditions of speech-song in Judaism, Islam and Christianity build on the fact that long passages of text are most easily memorised when they're accompanied by melody. The transmission of religious thought in the first few centuries AD relied on similar traditions of community learning and collective cultural immersion that the Songlines and the First Peoples of Australia knew so well. The word is God: in cantillation, in chant, and in the declamation of the Koran, the song is God, and God is song.

PIECE #5

HILDEGARD OF BINGEN
(1098–1179)

ORDO VIRTUTUM

Rupertsberg, Germany, 1151

If the word of God is sung, the words of the Devil definitely are not: in Hildegard of Bingen's morality play, *Ordo Virtutum* ('The Rite of the Virtues'), the Devil – the only male part in the text and the music – is denied the possibility of using his singing voice. In Hildegard's twelfth-century musical theology, music's essential Godliness is unavailable to the forces of darkness, so, in performance, the Devil's rude, brute words of temptation are in stark contrast to the chants and hymns that the Virtues sing. The Virtues perform as a chorus, collectively, but each is also personified individually, as characters including Obedience, Faith and Hope: they are the spiritual guards that the central character, Anima, must call on. Anima is the soul whose temptation, resistance and salvation creates the drama of *Ordo Virtutum*, and it's her journey that we all go on as listeners to any performance of this morality play – the first work of musical drama by a named author in history.

Ordo Virtutum was made to be performed by Hildegard's nuns and her spiritual community. Hildegard was the catalyst behind the words and the music, when she was the Abbess of Rupertsberg, after moving with her nuns from Disibodenberg in 1151. This is the longest work of Hildegard's ecstatic monody (single lines of chant and melody) that survives. It's one of the creative centrepieces that reveals the intensity of her life lived in spiritual service and revelation.

Hildegard's work is a uniquely all-encompassing universe of thought, expression and feeling. She worked not only in the musical life of the abbeys she led in Germany, but as an artist, poet and musician, as well as gardener, medical expert, spiritual leader – and politically savvy negotiator of the patriarchal hierarchies of her Church. What she called her 'visions', her spiritual epiphanies, were recorded in her illuminated volume, *Scivias* ('Know the Ways'). Modern medical science thinks her visions coincided with the pain and transformed consciousness of migraines. In these heightened states of awareness and anguish, she confided her experiences to the anchoress Jutta and to Volmar, her tutor and amanuensis. Volmar was the only significant male presence at the abbey, and he was likely the first performer of the role of the Devil in *Ordo Virtutum*. All of the other roles were written for and taken by her nuns, and the Hildegard scholar Honey Meconi is confident that the part of the Queen of the Virtues, Humility, could have been intended by Hildegard for herself to play.

The drama of *Ordo Virtutum* is a version of the stories of diabolical temptation that Hildegard and her community knew so well from scripture. But in the Devil's granting of Anima all that her soul could want – 'whoever wants to follow me, I will give them all they desire!' – there's a prefiguring of the later German story of Faust, and in every subsequent story and musical drama about the false dreams of worldly fulfilment promised by a trickster devil or Mephisto. In *Ordo Virtutum*, the drama progresses towards Anima's epiphany that the Virtues are her true home, yet she feels unworthy after having left them to follow the Devil's temptation – 'I stink of the wounds that the age-old serpent has made gangrenous', she sings, in Hildegard's fearlessly vivid language. Yet it's Anima's acknowledgement of her sin that saves her, defying the Devil. She physically fights him with the Virtues alongside her, and the Devil is bound, his power sealed.

Hildegard's final words and music in the epilogue of *Ordo Virtutum* are about a salvation that comes through a confrontation with and acceptance of sin, not its avoidance. 'Now remember that the fullness which was made in the beginning need not have grown dry ... it wearies me that all my limbs are exposed to mockery: Father, behold, I am showing you my wounds'.

These are sentiments of profoundly human connection that reach across the millennia. Hildegard's artistic visions, recorded in text and image, contain startlingly vivid depictions of the pain of revelation and the agony of the human soul coming to terms with both its sinfulness and its hard-won divinity.

And that essential humanity finds even more vivid expression in the music she writes for the words of *Ordo Virtutum*. Like everything she composed, the music is made of single lines of melody and chant sung in unison by the voices. But Hildegard finds so much variety in the way her melodic lines fly free of human time. She creates a stark ecstasy in her music that runs through you as a blade of pure feeling.

In performances today, Hildegard's morality play is reinterpreted by medieval specialists and contemporary performers who come up with their own creative solutions to the inevitable differences between how *Ordo Virtutum* might have been performed in Rupertsberg in the twelfth century and our own time. That space is where the life of the music lies, in its openness and its invitation to performers: it 'reaches you its hand', just as the final words of *Ordo Virtutum* urge human beings to reach out to God.

PIECE #6

DIES IRAE PLAINCHANT

Europe, c. 1200

It's the most quoted musical symbol of fateful terror, of human frailty in the face of divine retribution, across Western classical popular culture: the opening few notes of the Dies Irae plainchant. '*Dies Irae, dies illa*' – 'day of wrath, that awful day': it's a chant whose text became part of the Roman Catholic Requiem Mass, since it describes the Last Judgement, when the Second Coming turns nature into supernature, when the dead will be raised, and every soul weighed to face heaven or hellfire. It's also a text that's full of sonic images as part of its divine fury: '*Tuba mirum, spargen sonum*', the third verse begins: 'the trumpet, with astounding blasts echoing over the sepulchres of the whole world, shall compel all before the throne'.

Composers such as Mozart and Verdi have taken these words as their cue to find the most savage sonic dramatisation they can for the words of the Dies Irae in their Requiems, from 1791 and 1874 respectively: Mozart unleashes a tempest of D minor for his orchestra and choir, and turns the Tuba Mirum into a solo for trombone that starts with reassuring solidity before the voices announce their doubt and fear in the face of the coming judgement. Verdi's Dies Irae is the most single-mindedly terrifying music he ever composed, a maelstrom of minor-key intensity in which the singers don't so much sing as scream and wail their agonies, as a chorus of already-damned sinners, while the orchestra is ripped apart by its own violence, with a savage off-beat bass drum. Verdi stages those trumpets that call the sinners to judgement as a moment of pure orchestral theatre, when the on-stage trumpeters are amplified by four more of them playing behind the concert platform, as if sounding from the vaults of the throne of God.

Yet neither Mozart nor Verdi use the tune of the old chant itself. What's so special about the Dies Irae melody, is that, more than any of the other thousands of chants in the Christian liturgy, it has become a fatalistic earworm for an entire civilisation over nearly a millennium. The first eight notes are the ones that count. They set the words '*Dies Irae, dies illa*', and whether they were composed by St Gregory in the seventh century, Bernard of Clairvaux in the twelfth, or Bonaventure in the thirteenth century, they have stuck to Western culture ever since.

On the face of it, the tune lacks the obvious drama of Mozart or Verdi's versions. Yet just those eight notes for those four words have a power that embodies their essence – the resignation of human frailty when faced with God's infallibility. The pitches weave a snake-like path from the minor third of the scale down to the home note. And that tonic pitch is repeated after being arrived at through the arcane sound of the flattened rather than the sharp seventh of the scale. Imagine Julie Andrews getting from 'ti' to 'do' in *The Sound of Music* not with a joyful sense of arrival, but an out-of-tune world-weariness – that's the effect, to our ears, of this flattened note. The Dies Irae chant is a performance of musical fate in action.

That's why it has become an icon for composers and artists who want to communicate instantly to their audiences that they, or their characters, are in a losing battle with destiny and with divine retribution. It's why the Phantom of the Opera has the notes of the chant pinned to his wall in Gaston Leroux's novel, while Oscar Wilde was inspired to compose a sonnet on hearing the Dies Irae sung in the Sistine Chapel. When Hector Berlioz uses the chant in the finale of his Symphonie Fantastique in 1830, it's blared out in the brass, it's twisted and tortured in the woodwinds, and it turns into a grotesque and terrifying can-can that extinguishes the life of the hero of the symphony.

No classical composer was as obsessed with the Dies Irae chant as Sergei Rachmaninoff, since the melody stalks his entire compositional life, from his First Symphony in the late nineteeth century, to his last piece in the 1940s, the 'Symphonic Dances'. Rachmaninoff dances with fate and seems, finally, to transcend it in the playfulness with which he uses it at the end. The tune creates a more straightforward horror when Wendy Carlos has a voice of deep, synthesised uncanniness intone the Dies Irae as Jack Nicholson and his family make their way to the Overlook Hotel in the opening of Stanley Kubrick's *The Shining* (1980), and Stephen Sondheim uses it for horrific thrills in the bloodiest musical ever to appear on Broadway, *Sweeney Todd* in 1979, in which 'The Ballad of Sweeney Todd' uses the Dies Irae as the Demon Barber of Fleet Street's murderous theme tune, his *memento mori*.

From religious devotion to irresistible psychological torment: the Dies Irae chant has become a *leitmotif* of existential terror in the Western imagination, a piece whose resonance is only amplified with each new context and in each new encounter with musical fate.

PIECE #7

PÉROTIN (ACTIVE AROUND 1200)

VIDERUNT OMNES

Paris, Notre-Dame Cathedral, c. 1200

Notre-Dame vaulted Gothic majesty was conceived not only as an architectural wonder, but an acoustic marvel, and that symbiosis inspired what became the single most seismic evolution in the development of Western music in the twelfth and thirteenth centuries. Those new sounds emerge in concert with the construction of the space. In the decades before 1260, when the cathedral reached its first stage of completion, the composers of the Notre-Dame school established techniques of combining many different voices at the same time in vocal polyphony – literally 'many-voicedness' – in ways that musical culture is still indebted to, but has never surpassed.

Voices singing different music at the same time: what's new about that? Singing together, making music together, as modern humans have done since roughly 100,000 BC, means that different voices have been singing different lines, melodies and harmonies simultaneously in countless lost repertoires of musicking. But for the Western imagination, this long moment of development by the late 1,100s is consecrated through the way the music is written down, notated and transmitted as a repertoire. As the Ancient Greeks had already developed a similar system, the idea of writing down how music sounded was not new, and Indian, Chinese and Korean cultures already had their own specific methods of music notation. In India, the earliest notations go back to the second millennium BC; in China, they are roughly two thousand years old. The oldest surviving complete piece of notation is the *Hymn to Nikkal* from the *Hurrian Songs*, discovered in the ancient Syrian city of Ugarit, dating from 1400 BC. But, in Europe, it was how this idea became a relatively fixed way of communicating musical ideas from one community to another, from one place to another, from one group of singers to another, that was so significant. This era of notational common practice, which is still the same system that Western musical notation uses today – with horizontal parallel lines to denote musical time, and note-heads positioned at different heights to communicate the pitches the voices should sing at – was the consolidated innovation that the composers at Notre-Dame could take advantage of by the twelfth century.

And this is the moment, for composers in the West at least, when the Pandora's Box of polyphony cracks open, allowing many voices to sing at the same time, producing new kinds of musical motion, from one harmony to another, from one texture to another, to create everything from consonant relationships between the voices to sounds of dissonant entanglement. A whole world of musical, expressive and human possibility is revealed that previous repertoires of monody had kept closed. These ideas – using notation to explore realms of thought, idea and feeling that improvisational and oral cultures don't do in the same way, and the possibilities of having multiple musical parts, of instruments as well as voices, performing simultaneously – are the musical keys that unlock much of the rest of the music in this book, and it's a seismic shock whose consequences musical culture is still indebted to, and still reeling from.

Back to Viderunt Omnes: this piece is only identified as the work of Pérotin – Magister Perotinus – thanks to the testimony of a student from England who was at Notre-Dame in the later thirteenth century, an individual ironically only known today as Anonymous IV. Pérotin's piece is a multi-dimensional efflorescence for four voices, in which the liturgical plainchant of Viderunt Omnes (Latin for 'all shall see') is used as the basis for a flight of meditation and imagination. The text was sung in the liturgy on Christmas Day: 'All the ends of the earth have seen / the Salvation of our God / Rejoice in the Lord, all lands'. Yet in Pérotin's piece, the text isn't set in a way that's supposed to make it comprehensible. Instead, the words are extended via techniques of melisma, singing many notes on the same syllable. In Pérotin's heightened musical setting, that means singing for 30 seconds and more before moving to the next syllable of the text, and by having the chant sung at different speeds at the same time. The text, the melody and the spiritual meaning of the chant would have been so well understood by Pérotin's singers and his intended audiences that the music can fly of the words in an ecstasy of invention.

Pérotin's work mirrors the elaborate ornamentation of the Gothic architecture of Notre-Dame, in which the forms of pillars and vaults and their over-worked decoration of stone-work and imagery cannot be separated. In Notre-Dame, the form is the ornamentation, and vice-versa. That obsessive working of every surface inside the cathedral is also what accounts for the space's acoustic richness, as the sounds of Pérotin's voices are reflected with infinite subtleties of resonance across its improbable geometries.

Pérotin's glorious complexity in the handful of works that are now ascribed to him builds on the achievement of the founder of Notre-Dame's polyphony, Léonin. He is another figure who emerges not through signing his work but through the testimony of Anonymous IV, who tells us that Léonin is the principal author of the *Magnus Liber Organi*, the 'great book of organum' of early polyphony, published in the early thirteenth century. Léonin's two-voice pieces show the invention of what he could do with plainchant once he freed himself from the monody, the single-voice, of the earlier tradition. You could sing the chant at different speeds, you could add an improvisational-sounding line above the plainchant, or you could come up with rhythmic and melodic games between the voices. The *Magnus Liber Organi* is also the place where Pérotin's later three- and four-voiced pieces appear: the book's significance is the establishment of writing down melody and rhythm in ways that allow us to feel the voices of Léonin and Pérotin as individuals communicating with us from nearly a millennium ago so that 'all the ends of the earth' can share in their innovations.

And in the re-opened Notre-Dame after the fire that nearly destroyed the cathedral in 2019, their music goes on reverberating in the place it was intended to resound, for their time, and for ours: a polyphony that's still Western music's present tense.

PIECE #8

COMTESSA DE DIA (*c.* 1175–1212)

'A CHANTAR M'ER'

Southern France, c. 1200

But at exactly the same time, across the twelfth and thirteenth centuries, further south in Occitania – south of the Loire, extending down to today's Catalonia and west to the Piedmont Alps – there were singers establishing just as important a repertoire in secular song. The history of the troubadours spans the period during the Crusades in the Occitan courts, inspiring songs about love from afar, chivalry, and courtly romance.

The majority of roughly 2,500 lyrics in Occitan that survive from the troubadour's heyday of around 1,100–1,350 are by men. They established the expression of courtly love that defined ideas of romance that everything from nineteenth-century art-song to Hollywood rom-coms are still indebted to: a love from afar, a male longing for an idealised female beloved who remains always out of reach, a love all the sweeter for being unrequited, which never has to face the realities of relationship or the messy consequences of the world. Bernart de Ventadorn, who left the most complete poems and songs of any troubadour, praised the generosity and beauty of the grand ladies who employed him. Bernart fell in love with Marguerite de Turenne, the wife of his patron, Viscount Eble III. He turned Marguerite into his ideal of physical and spiritual beauty, comparing her to the seasons, his feelings to forces of nature. In love with her, yet never able to possess her – the perfect inspiration for a male troubadour.

But these songs, so often addressed to or about women, were also composed by female singers and composers: the troubairitz. While there are 450 male troubadours whose work is recorded, there are just 23 troubairitz in historical records, with up to 46 lyrics composed by them – although there were surely more singers, composers and songs in the troubairtiz tradition than history now knows.

To be a courtly troubairitz meant, like the troubadours, that you probably belonged to the nobility rather than the lower social strata where mere professional musicians resided. And that also meant that you were sufficiently well-established in society to be able to sing about the subjects you most wanted to. For the troubairitz, that included glosses on love and longing according to the poetic conventions of the time, but it also meant singing about politics: Gormonda de Monpeslier sang about her desire to murder the heretics within Occitania in the early thirteenth century. But most importantly, some of the surviving troubairitz's poems and songs subvert the male gaze of the troubadours and the patriarchal conventions of the court. In Bieiris de Romans's lyric, 'Na Maria, pretz e fina valors' ('Lady Maria, in your merit and distinction'), from the first half of the thirteenth century, she sings as a woman to another woman, in lyrics that have been interpreted as expressions both of deferential respect and erotic desire.

The single troubairitz song, 'A chantar m'er', which has been preserved as a melody as well as a text, surviving in 15 different manuscripts, is by the Comtessa de Dia. Her biography is scant: probably the daughter of the Count Isoard II of the town of Die, she was married to William II of Poitiers, but her songs were written for her lover, a troubadour himself, Raimbaut of Orange, who ruled over regions of Southern France.

In 'A chantar m'er' ('I must sing of what I do not want'), she writes a tune that's a heartbreaking keening, both hopeful and hopeless. The text is about the betrayal of her lover, set to a melodic line that descends and descends again to find a troubled acceptance in each of its verses: 'Best beloved ... You are arrogant in word and deed towards me ... But you ... are so wise / That you will ... remember our pact'.

'A chantar m'er' is the first secular song composed by a woman to have survived in Western history. It's a song that cuts through the courtly conventions of the troubadours, daring to express real-life passion, anger and vividness. In their intensity, the lyrics and the melody are a fierce reclaiming of the Comtessa de Dia's own subjective passion in a context in which women were supposed to receive affection and emotion, not act on their own account. In the final verse, the Comtessa sings: 'I send this song down to you / So that it would be a messenger / I want to know ... Why you are so cruel and savage to me'. This is an acknowledgement of the power and purpose of her composition to express those feelings, and to be a 'messenger' to her lover. Whether or not her message was heeded in her lifetime – by Raimbaut? or was this impassioned lyric and plangently unforgettable melody intended for someone else? – it is certainly listened to by us today. Her message has carried through the centuries, and when we hear this song, we hear the Comtessa's voice, and the voice of the troubairitz, finding our hearts with rapier precision more than 800 years later.

PIECE #9

PRINCE MANGKUNEGRA IV OF SURAKARTA

KETAWANG PUSAPAWARNA

('KINDS OF FLOWERS')

Java, Indonesia, before 1881

This is one of the pieces that Carl Sagan chose to represent humanity's music on The Golden Record, the discs that take sounds of our civilisation to deep space on board both the Voyager spacecraft. Launched in 1977, Voyager 1 is now 15 billion miles from the sun, and its nearest encounter with potential lifeforms will come in 40,000 years, when it passes within a mere 1.6 light years of the constellation Camelopardalis.

And if those celestial civilisations can work out how to actually play The Golden Record, they will hear the gamelan of the court of Pura Paka Alaman on Java. 'Kinds of Flowers' was written by the late nineteeth-century Prince Mangkunegra IV in honour of his wives and concubines. And in the performance recorded at the Pura Paka court in 1971 on its priceless eighteenth-century gamelan, all of us here on Earth can hear a tradition in action in one of the Javanese gamelan's repertory pieces, in which choirs of gongs and voices mark musical time in ways that are both sensual and cosmic. Like any gamelan ensemble, the one at the Pura Paka court, made of bell-shaped gongs and metallic percussion, makes a sound that's uniquely resonant and rich, tuned in scales that are only found in Indonesian culture, which seem to create halos of sound above the instruments as they play, turning reverberation into a physical feeling as no other ensemble of instruments on the planet does.

The cosmology and the physicality of any gamelan performance is inherent in its origins. Religious mythology says that the first gamelan was conjured by the god Sang Hyang Guru in 230 AD. He was the ruler of Java, sitting atop Maendra mountain, and he needed to communicate with Indonesia's other gods, so created the first gong, adding two others to create richer messages, and founding the first gamelan ensemble.

The gongs you hear in *Ketawang Pusapawarna* are playing according to the cycles of time and texture that define the way all of the instruments and voices of any gamelan ensemble function. Instead of imagining time as a flow from beginning to end, or as a progression from one state towards another – the way that Western music so often imagines time to work – the interlocking cycles of melody and rhythm in gamelan repertoires, like *Ketawang Pusapawarna*, embody another idea completely.

In gamelan, musical time is made of a series of spirals that repeat in layers on top of one another. The patterns loop, so time moves in loops as well: not towards a single definitive goal, since the 'goal' is an immersion in a state of being. Gamelan's musical time is a pool of resonances to dive into, not a river leading inexorably forward. In *Ketawang Pusapawarna*, you hear the interaction of the longest cycles of time – sounded by the lowest and biggest gong – with the faster cycles of the higher-pitched gongs and voices. That marking of deeper time, contrasted with shorter, higher patterns, is a beautiful reflection of acoustic reality, in which lower frequencies pulse more slowly, with fewer frequencies per second, than higher pitches do.

That expression of a unique world of time is one of the reasons that this gamelan performance was one of Carl

Sagan's favourites on The Golden Record, and it's also why gamelan's repertoires have been so influential on Western composers from the nineteenth century onwards. Gamelan inspired many musicians to break out of the straitjacket of the march of Western time, like Claude Debussy, who heard gamelan at the Great Exhibition in Paris, and whose music was never the same; or Benjamin Britten, who travelled to Indonesia and composed his ballet *The Prince of the Pagodas*; and Steve Reich, whose pulsing minimalism in the late twentieth and twenty-first centuries is another revelation of music as interwoven cycles of time.

Born from a god on a mountaintop and now flung into interstellar space: gamelan and its repertoires, like *Ketawang Pusapawarna*, gives us mortals on Earth a glimpse of those bigger spirals of chiming musical space-time.

PIECE #10

ANONYMOUS, _c._ 1450

'L'HOMME ARMÉ'

JOSQUIN (_c._ 1450/55–1521)

MASSES ON
'L'HOMME ARMÉ'

France, before 1502

'L'*homme armé*' is an anonymously written tune of secular conquest – 'The armed man should be feared – which nonetheless became the basis for dozens of sacred masses composed in the fifteenth and sixteenth century, the tune around which the liturgical text was woven. The effect is both ironic and profound: a soldier's song of human hubris, used as the centre of music made for divine contemplation, a fusion of human time and sacred time, a meditation on church, state and power.

And of the scores of settings from composers in the High Renaissance in Europe, from Guillaume Dufay in the 1450s to Palestrina in the late 1500s, it's the two masses on '*L'homme armé*' by Josquin Despez that stand out. But as well as the question of imitating and, compositionally speaking, besting his predecessors, the question remains: why? Why did Josquin use this bellicose secular street-song instead of the vast repertoire of liturgical plainchants that every European composer knew, working under the patronage of the Catholic Church?

The tune and text of '*L'homme armé*' emerges in printed sources in the late fifteenth century, but it's still a moot point whether the tune was written by one of the early '*L'homme armé*' mass composers themselves, or whether it was taken down from how it circulated on streets and in pubs, like the tavern which was actually called the 'Maison l'homme armé' near where Guillaume Dufay lived. Did Dufay hear it there, write it down, and start the trend himself?

Whatever its origins, the popularity of 'L'homme armé' coincides with an era in Western Europe when fears of military powers from the East were justified: 'L'homme armé' becomes the go-to tune for God-fearing composers at the same time the Ottomans took Constantinople in 1453. The rest of its short text is about arming yourself in the face of the threat: 'Everywhere it has been proclaimed / That each man shall arm himself / With a coat of iron mail'.

The musical material of 'L'homme armé' makes it a fantastic fifteenth-century earworm. It's catchy, and curious, in how the stresses of the phrases are displaced across its quick, three-time metre; there's a defiant leap of an octave when the words tell the singers to equip themselves with their chain mail, and the repetition of the opening line at the end is a reminder of the fear that everyone ought to have in the face of this worldly threat. If the threat really is of this world: another interpretation of the 'armed man' is that he stands for the archangel St Michael, who protects Israel and battles Satan.

Those multiple meanings are only the start of the compositional matrix that Josquin composes for and around this tune in his two masses. He was one of the most famous and highly paid composers in Europe when he wrote these pieces, and Josquin takes the melody into places of polyphonic imagination that send up its seemingly simple call to arms. In the radically repurposed context of these mass settings, the tune isn't only expressively separated from its meaning – a mass sung in church isn't the best place to recruit soldiers to the anti-Ottoman cause – it's as if Josquin is showing his singers and his listeners that it doesn't matter how humble, secular and one-dimensional a melody might be, he can still use it as a catalyst for virtuosic musical invention. That's what you feel listening to the mind-melting mathematical complexity throughout Josquin's first 'L'homme armé' mass, in which the tune is sung in imitation and in rhythmic syncopation. And in the Agnus Dei movement of the second mass, the melody is simultaneously sung forward and backwards. In jaw-dropping moments like that, Josquin opens a soundworld that reaches forward into the musical modernism of our time.

Josquin's 'L'homme armé' takes a melody of bellicose impetuosity and pacifies it through sheer compositional inspiration. In the twentieth century and on the cusp of the twenty-first, the composers Peter Maxwell Davies and Karl Jenkins wrote their own masses using the 'L'homme armé' tune. In Jenkins's version, there's a plea for unity and peace in the mix of genres, languages and immediacy he creates. In contrast, Davies's biting satire, composed in 1971, stages a dissolution of the sacred into the profane, making a mirror of society's pretensions to make peace while preparing for war. They are powerful in their own right, yet Josquin's musical invention in his masses remains miraculous, repurposing the 'L'homme armé' for spiritual and musical transcendence. Do not fear the armed man: exorcise him in a mass.

PIECE #11

BELL PATTERN

STANDARD PATTERN/BEMBÉ

Sub-Saharan Africa, to Cuba and the rest of the world from the sixteenth century onwards

The origins of the bell patterns in the music of sub-Saharan Africa begin with the Bantu migrations in the continent, starting around 2000 BC, and the iron-making technologies they developed. That metalwork included the cowbells that are the original bell-instruments these rhythmic patterns were played upon. And what's become the so-called 'standard pattern' of Sub-Saharan music, a 12-beat rhythmic set, has taken over much of the world from the Caribbean to South America, in the wake of the traumatic history of slavery and the African diaspora, since the early sixteenth century.

So what is this pattern, and why has it become so dominant a piece of musical cultures across the world? The way it works is to simultaneously set up and cut across a regular grid of time. The notes you hear on the bell, the drum or the body percussion, in cultures from the drum orchestras of the Ewe people in West Africa to the Candomblé rituals in Brazil, make an irresistibly syncopated dance. Seven of the twelve quavers in the pattern are sounded, in a grouping that goes like this: pa – pa – pa pa – pa – pa – pa, looping and repeating ad infinitum. You can imagine the twelve quavers split into four groups of three as a guiding principle underneath the notes you hear, but that grid is never played, so the rhythm is never reduced to a regular four-square tattoo.

Instead, this pattern is complex in its syncopations, but visceral in how it feels. Because it invites you to parse the pulses in many different ways, it sets up a dance of musical perception, how we interpret it in our brains and our hearing, before any other element – voices, instruments, melodies – is added. The rhythm creates the sensation that it's grooving against itself. To get the standard pattern down as a rhythm that you so much as tap out on your table is to be moving with it, dancing with it. The pattern is the embodied expression of freedom, as the rhythm bounces across divisions of pulse and metre.

And the standard pattern is only the start: it's the rhythmic seed of countless variations of it that are the foundations of entire genres of music, from Congo to Zambia, Nigeria to Haiti, and it's also the root of the most common syncopation in pop music, from rock and roll to hip hop, from jazz to Afrobeat. That's a grouping of 3+3+2 quavers against a background metre of 4+4, creating the feeling of a syncopated triplet. This is the irregular parsing of time that gives so much Western pop music its groove, even if it's a simplified version of the standard pattern's richer and more complex essence.

The standard pattern is also a piece in its own right: after studying in Ghana, the American composer Steve Reich wrote *Clapping Music*, in which rhythm is all there is: the piece is made of a 12-quaver pattern that two players, using nothing but their clapping hands, repeat against one another, looping the pattern against itself until they arrive back together in unison. Reich's piece is credited as his own creation, but it's really just another place in which the standard pattern finds its home, everywhere from the post-war avant-garde to centuries-old traditions of Cuban dances to the millennia-old heritage of African drumming.

PIECE #12

GIOVANNI PIERLUIGI DA PALESTRINA (1525–1594)

MISSA PAPAE MARCELLI

Rome, 1562

And so, the legend goes, it came to pass that, in the year 1562, Italy's most famous composer, the person who had brought a style and a musical era to fruition, saved all future composers from a fate worse than death. Thanks to the diktats of the cardinals of the Council of Trent, the censoring of musical creativity would have been catastrophic, were it not for the work of one man, Giovanni Pierluigi da Palestrina.

Among the conclusions that it took the Council of Trent 17 years to reach was that vocal music for the Catholic Church was becoming too florid, too complicated, and too obsessed with its own virtuosity instead of the purity of the communication of the Word. It's easier to understand a text when it's sung by solo voices singing one melodic line, which is the way that plainchant works, rather than having six voices curlicue around one another singing the text at different speeds and times. That was the kind of richness that Palestrina and his fellow sixteenth-century composers had developed in Italy. Too much, said the cardinals; too hubristic, too full of human vanity and not enough puritan divinity, they thought.

What could Palestrina do to convince them they were wrong? Palestrina had to write the most important mass setting of his life in what became the *Missa Papae Marcelli*. At the height of his powers, in his mid-forties, having been *maestro di cappella* – responsible for running the choirs, and all the music-making – at St Peter's in Rome, Palestrina knew how to negotiate the papal powers as much as he knew how to write vocal music that took the intertwining voices of polyphony to new heights of expressive power and compositional density.

The *Missa Papae Marcelli* is the only mass setting of Palestrina's to bear the name of a dedicatee, Pope Marcellus II, who reigned for just 23 days before his death in 1555. But we know that Marcellus's programme for reform would have reflected his sensitivity to music. In his temporally tiny tenure, Marcellus expressed his desire that the singers should modulate their singing according to the time of day they were performing, while also insisting on the primacy of textual comprehension. His successor, Paul IV, fired Palestrina from St Peter's along with other married singers in the choir, thinking they were potential sources of scandal. Palestrina had good reason to commemorate the musically enthusiastic Marcellus when he came to write this mass of masses in 1562.

Put all of those elements together – papal intolerance, the Council of Trent's strictures, Palestrina's professional pride – and you have the makings of historical and musical myth. Palestrina becomes an artistic liberation fighter, struggling to continue a tradition that he had spent his life perfecting, and, in the triumphant composition of the *Missa Papae Marcelli*, convincing the papacy that he was right and they were wrong. Here was a mass in which the words of the Creed were easily understood, but also in which Palestrina could let his gifts flower for the glory of God and the Church.

Palestrina doesn't fold and give the cardinals what they want. He doesn't debase his art to win approval. The music of the Mass for Pope Marcellus skilfully blends the uncompromised ornamental brilliance of polyphony at its richest, with six voices weaving in and out of each other in movements like the Kyrie and the Agnus Dei. But Palestrina ensures that the movements with the most words – the Gloria and the Creed, the Credo – are significantly clearer. To do that, Palestrina doesn't just write the simplest music he could, with one note to each syllable, and everyone singing together. Instead, he groups the voices so they sing in a relay. The text is always audible, but they seem to be inhabiting different musical dimensions of time and space at once.

On 28 April 1565, a colloquy of cardinals convened to look over settings of the mass, including Palestrina's, to see if the Council of Trent's laws had been obeyed. Palestrina passed, and polyphony lived to fight another day, another decade, and another half century and more. Palestrina would return to St Peter's in 1571 for the rest of his life, dying in 1594. Did the *Missa Papae Marcelli* save his fate, and that of every other composer of church music at the time? On its own, probably not. But the reputation and image of Palestrina, musical and creative freedom fighter, lives on with his music – as it should.

PIECE #13

MADDALENA CASULANA (1544–1590)

IL PRIMO LIBRO
DI MADRIGALI

Venice, 1568

Maddalena Casulana's first book of madrigals is dedicated to Isabella de' Medici, in 1568, when the composer was in her mid-twenties, with the following words: 'These first fruits of mine ... show the world (to the degree that is granted to me in this profession of music) the foolish error of men, who believe themselves the masters of high intellectual gifts, which – it seems to them – cannot be equally common among women.' As the first named female author of a collection of music to be printed and published in Western history, Casulana had every right – as had so many anonymous female composers before her – to show the patriarchies of musical taste, judgement and power the reality of the distribution of talent across the sexes.

The fact that she had to write these words at all is testament at once to her creative assurance, and to the situations of professional and personal insecurity that the women of her society in Northern Italy faced – not least by Isabella de' Medici herself, who would be murdered on the instructions of her husband and brother just a few years later.

Casulana's work was heralded in her time, and performed by the most famous composers on the continent – Orlando Lassus, for example, conducted her music in Bavaria. But a combination of historical myopia and prejudice has meant that her music has been unsung and undiscovered until very recently. Her book of five-voice madrigals was unearthed in

Russia in 2022, and sung and recorded for the first time in over 400 years by Laurie Stras and the singers of the Fieri Consort. It's music of delirious poetic and expressive fantasy, in which Casulana's place at the summit of sixteenth-century songwriters is assured, her music at last available for future generations to explore.

One of the madrigals of the first book, written for four voices, powerfully reveals Casulana's unique voice, and her uncanny understanding of how music can enhance the meaning and emotional drama of a text in a piece that lasts less than a couple of minutes. In her setting of Sannazaro's poem '*Morir non può il mio cuore*' ('My heart cannot die'), she finds a musical ache from the very opening notes: searching, unpredictable leaps and dissonances that land you, in a new harmonic region, just a few seconds into the piece.

The words of the poem imagine how a lover wants to kill her own heart, out of spite for how she has been treated, 'But it cannot be pulled out of your breast / Where it has been dwelling for a long time'. Casulana saves her most breathtaking musical image for the final lines, in which the scorned lover's death-pact is revealed: 'And if I killed it, as I wish / I know that you would die'. Casulana sets this shocking idea to a rising sequence of tortuous dissonances, the most voluptuous yet horrifying sounds in the song. That's a musical and poetic sensation she repeats, so we're left in no doubt of the seriousness of purpose of the singer of these words, their despair and pain. There are 'high intellectual gifts' here: even more powerful is the devastating expressive intensity of Casulana's musical imagination.

PIECE #14

CLAUDIO MONTEVERDI
(1567–1643)

L'ORFEO

Mantua, 1607

This is not an 'opera', even though that's how Monteverdi's epic setting of the fable of Orpheus is performed and thought of today: he performed and published *L'Orfeo* as a *favola in musica*, a 'fable in music', for its first performances for the Duke of Mantua in 1607. Yet that original description fits the expressive and generic project of this piece, the most fully-fledged revelation of the experimental powers of music drama that composers in Northern Italy were exploring at the start of the seventeenth century.

The true pioneers of what became opera were Jacopo Peri and Giulio Caccini in Florence, who, at the end of the previous century turned *intermedii*, musical scenes between the spoken acts of plays, into dramas with music in their own right, and the seeds of a new genre were sown. The proto-operatic project was all about unleashing the power of music to underscore and dramatise stories in new ways. This new type of storytelling with music insisted on the primacy of the drama, the action, and the expression of the text instead of previous generations of vocal polyphony, like Palestrina's, in which the text is as much a basis for musical invention as a site of emotional revelation.

Monteverdi, who'd been working for the Duke of Mantua since the early 1590s, absorbed all the lessons of his predecessors, and in working with the subject of Orpheus, he had a ready-made drama that's all about the existential power of music. He wasn't the first to have that that dramatic idea, as both Peri and Caccini had told the story of Orpheus and Euridice in previous pieces, but Monteverdi supersedes them in the richness and immediacy of *L'Orfeo*, and how exquisitely he uses all of the available resources of the Mantuan court to sound out the story's regions of pastoral idylls, the pitiless denizens of hell, and the intervention of heaven to tell this ever-resonant love story.

Orpheus is the original musician of the Western imagination in Greek myth. The power of his voice and his virtuosity with the lyre are the enchantments that convince Charon to take him over the River Styx to Hades to plead for the life of his Euridice, who has been killed by a snake bite in the fields of Thrace. Orpheus' irresistible musical petition in front of the King and Queen of the Underworld, Pluto and Prosperina, convinces them to send Euridice back to him – on the condition that he does not look back to see her as they leave Hades. But Orpheus can't resist: he has to know if she is following him, and for this transgression, he is tortured to death in a frenzy by the Maenads.

At least, that's the classical version of the myth, but the ending of Monteverdi's *L'Orfeo* has Apollo save Orpheus, taking him to the stars, where he will see Euridice's likeness again. Monteverdi's opera ends with an earthy dance of joy, connecting the pleasure of the players and singers on stage with the courtly audience who paid for their entertainment. In between the fanfare that *L'Orfeo* opens with, calling his listeners to attention, and that final dance, Monteverdi's five acts make a stunning case for this hybrid form of all the arts (that's the root of the word 'opera', literally translated from Italian as 'works') and how it can define new regions of feeling with an embodiment and an empathy that are new in the Western imagination.

Monteverdi builds on the dramatic and musical conventions of his time, rather than innovating them. The power is in how he puts all of the elements of vocal setting, instrumental imagination and dramatic pacing together. He uses the three main groups of his huge, 40-strong instrumentarium – brass, strings and woodwind, and continuo (Baroque music's rhythms and bass section) in ways that his audiences would recognise. He colours the Underworld with low, blaring, ominous brass, and the rasping sounds of the portable organ, known as the regal; he uses high strings and woodwind for the pastoral scenes of Thrace, and deploys the continuo to colour the solo recitatives and arias for the characters, which carry the drama. But Monteverdi gives broad brushtrokes for his orchestration rather than prescribing which instruments should be used exactly when: he leaves that in the hands of his trusted interpreters, who would know how best to use their scale and variety to amplify the expressive power and potential of each scene.

It's that fluidity and generosity of Monteverdi's composition that's most staggering about *L'Orfeo* today. Performed a handful of times before his death in 1643, but forgotten for centuries, only to be revived in variously mutilated editions in the nineteenth and early twentieth centuries, *L'Orfeo* is now a piece that extends its invitation to all of us. In arias like Orfeo's plea to Charon in Act 3, Monteverdi finds an immediacy of word-setting in which you hear the emotion vibrate in sympathy with the text. And in the despair of Euridice's aria, when she realises that Orpheus will lose her and consign her to hell because he loves her too much, there's a rawness of expression in which you're not aware of all the artifices of composition and performance that have created this moment, only the sucker punch of pure feeling.

That's what's new, for 1607 – and for all time, about Monteverdi's *L'Orfeo*. And that's the distilled magic of what opera can do to us. *L'Orfeo* is a work of works, a multimedia spectacle – a fable made of music, about music – that opens up a world of wonder in the relationship between words, singing and drama that every composer of music theatre ever since has been exploring. They're all compositional Orpheuses, following in Monteverdi's footsteps to those mysterious, marvellous regions where music-drama is born: journeys to hell and heaven, and all the lands in between.

PIECE #15

FRANCESCA CACCINI
(1587–AFTER 1641)

LA LIBERAZIONE
DI RUGGIERO

Florence, 1625

In Florence, at the Medici court in the early 1600s, Francesca Caccini took the project of the operatic art form still further, not only as a composer, but in her life as an artistic polymath: a professional singer, promoter, teacher, lutenist and poet. Her father, the composer Giulio Caccini, was one of the founders of the new opera, and he formed an all-female singing group in Florence, a sort of superstar Von Trapp family group for the Medici court, called the Donne di Caccini, in which Francesca sang alongside her sisters, her mother, and her father's pupils. Francesca's brilliance across all domains of music-making, and her essential place at the heart of Florentine cultural life, meant that she rose to become the court's highest-paid musician. Francesca was Tuscany's musical embodiment of the ideal of female excellence, at a time when Tuscan royalty was controlled by Christina of Lorraine: where Christina led, culture and court followed.

Francesca's surviving work as a composer, a generation after the experimentalism of her father, reveals both a consolidation and an enrichment of the innovations of the previous generation. The new commitment, embodied by the manifestos of the Florentine Camerata, a group that included her father, was to find a new musical freedom by being inspired by the power and drama of text and story. Immediacy of expression, rhetorical directness and emotional clarity were the new watchwords. In her *First Book of Music*, published in 1618, Francesca Caccini composed 36 monodies – single-voiced songs and scenes of sacred and secular music – that prove the principle in action.

It's one of the biggest losses of music history: of around 13 stage works she composed, only one survives, *La liberazione di Ruggiero* ('The Liberation of Ruggiero'). In the story, the knight Ruggiero is saved from the witchery of Alcina on her magical island where he is kept as her lover and where all her previous paramours have been magicked into exotic vegetation. This piece – the first opera that survives by a woman in Europe – was commissioned in 1625 by Maddalena of Austria, who had married Duke Cosimo of the Medicis. Maddalena needed a lavish entertainment for the visit of Crown Prince of Poland at her Florentine palace, since she was trying to marry her daughter to him.

The 38-year-old Caccini's response to the commission is tailored with decorous specificity in the opening prologue that addresses the royals directly, hoping that the evening's entertainment will create 'joyful sights for royal hearts'. But in the substance of the storytelling of her opera, she transcends Maddalena's politicking in how sharply she characterises her music for the sorcerers of good and evil, Melissa and Alcina, and Ruggiero, the knight who needs rescuing. She uses bespoke instrumentation and harmonies for each of them: flat keys and sonorous strings for Alcina's magical realms, as opposed to the sharp keys of Ruggiero's recitatives and arias, with his accompaniment of recorders, while Melissa – who cross-dresses as the god Atlus to disguise herself and save him – sings with bass instruments underneath her.

La liberazione is a music-drama that's composed by a woman with a female role as the saviour of the knight: the ultimate swapping and usurping of conventional gender roles. Ruggiero is in a bewitched torpor from which Melissa rescues him: she is the active heroine and he the passive bystander. The action is driven by the dynamism of the women in the story, and the unforgettably dramatic music that Caccini writes for them. Alcina's wounded pride and her genuine tenderness for Ruggiero at the centre of the second scene makes her a deeply sympathetic villain, not a one-dimensional sorceress, thanks to Caccini's music of nobility, dignity and quicksilver emotional change.

Caccini's success with her opera was greater than Maddalena's political machinations: despite the ballet for 24 horses that the evening's entertainment ended with at her palace in 1625, the Crown Prince of Poland chose Maddalena's niece instead of her daughter to marry. But he was so impressed with *La liberazione*, and its story of female-dominated drama, that he had it performed in Warsaw in 1628. Caccini's piece is the tip of an iceberg of lost operatic music that – here's hoping – historians may yet rediscover, because Caccini's life and music tell some of the most vital stories at the heart of seventeenth-century culture, politics and power.

PIECE #16

BARBARA STROZZI
(1619–1677)

'IL LAMENTO'

Venice, 1651

I'm going to tell you about just one of the more than 125 songs, cantatas and miniature music-dramas that Barbara Strozzi made in her life at the heart of Venetian musical culture. Unsupported by the conventions of church or court, she was the most published and most famous figure of a musical scene that flourished both underground – she was the only female musician admitted to otherwise all-male societies that debated and presented philosophy, politics and the arts – and in the full public glare of the echelons of Venetian aristocracy. Her father, Giulio Strozzi, belonged to one of the most culturally influential families in the city at a time when Venice was the continent's major hub of mercantilism, inspiring astonishing excess across the whole spectrum of the arts from architecture to painting, from sculpture to music. There was also an explosion of opera and music drama by the mid-seventeenth century, performed by professional musicians, who sold tickets to the merchants of Venice to come to their shows.

Barbara Strozzi didn't write any pieces called 'opera'. Yet everything she wrote and published – and no composer, female or male, had as much secular vocal music in print as she did at the time – is as dramatic, and operatic, in the unflinching emotional expression she virtuosically unleashes in music composed for her to perform herself in those secret societies that were at the vanguard of Venetian musical creativity.

The piece I've chosen comes from the earlier part of her life as a published composer: '*Il Lamento*' ('The Lament') from her Op. 2 collection, published in 1651. Like so many of her compositions, it doesn't fall into a straightforward category of 'song' or 'aria': her music is much more diverse and unpredictable than that, because what's most important for her is how composition dramatises and amplifies the power, imagery and political impact of the texts and stories she's setting. That's profoundly true in this lament for Henri, Marquis of Cinq-Mars, who was beheaded by Louis XIII in 1642 in France, supposedly for being part of a plot to murder one of his cardinals. Strozzi's lament turns Cinq-Mars into a ghost narrating the story of his life and death, just a few years after the terrible event that stained the river Rhône purple with blood. Strozzi would have known the rumour that, as Louis's favourite, Cinq-Mars was also the King's lover, and her response is music that's full of raw emotion and unfettered passion.

She doesn't write a single form or shape for this 12-minute-long scene, but a series of pieces that create a continuity through fearless emotional intensity. At its dark heart is a lamenting song, which is based on a descending bassline, the seventeenth century's *lingua franca* for despair, setting words in which the ghost of Henri remembers how the King put his 'gracious arm around my neck'. This is the very intimacy that consigned Henri to his fate, as the court swelled with jealousy, which would see the favourite destroyed. In the recitatives around these islands of song, Strozzi finds a language for the voice that gives full rein to the vertiginous tightrope of emotions the ghost is going through: recounting the horror of his execution, yet finding forgiveness for the King who loved him – and who killed him: Cinq-Mars accuses him 'of no crime other than that of excessive love'. Strozzi's music is composed for single voice and continuo, which today's performers can interpret as richly as they like, turning Strozzi's bassline and harmonic figures into a flowering for the instruments that she knew in Venice: strings, organ, lutes.

What Strozzi has made in this lament is a miniature opera, a vividly experimental *scena* in which she expresses a fearless psychology of emotion. The final image is overwhelming in its word-painting, and unsparing in its power: the king sees the dead Henri before him and weeps with repentance, as Strozzi turns a minor third into major, as if this act of contrition were somehow enough to atone for the murder of his beloved. It isn't: for the very last line of the poem – 'Paris trembles and the Seine grows dark' – Strozzi creates a terrifying tremulation on a harmony that's deliberately unresolved. She confronts us at the end of this lament with the trauma of Louis and Henri, and a love that burned so bright it had to be extinguished by the court, by the brute daylight of politics and plotting. Strozzi makes her lament a savagely honest honouring of forbidden love.

No other musician of her time dared to put her own musical body on the line like Strozzi. This was music for her to sing to those all-male power brokers of Venice's – and the world's – trade and politics. And she confronts them with the sound of a visceral sensuality and sheer compositional bravery that is an ongoing inspiration. When she performed this piece, she became Henri in his agony and his love; she became Louis in his pain and his shame; she became their aching memorial of lament.

And this is just one number of Strozzi's output. Every moment of her music is full of the same subtlety, sensitivity and psychological insight. Her music is a record of a life that was lived with similar intensity, in everything she achieved as a composer and musician, as a superstar of the light and the shadows of Venice's many social worlds. Strozzi's music speaks through the centuries more clearly than so much music of the time because she serves the drama of her words and her characters before anything else, making her stories our stories.

PIECE #17

CHANGE RINGING

THE TRADITION OF BELL RINGING AND ITS REPERTOIRES

England, seventeenth century

Tintinnalogia: that's the title of the 1668 publication that set down what bell-ringers in Britain – and England in particular – had been doing with the peals of bells in their church towers since around the start of the seventeenth century. This 'bell-ringing logic' was a scientific guide that set out the principles of how to effect some of the longest, loudest and most unmissable pieces of organised sound that the human imagination has ever come up with: the many arts and methods of Change Ringing, in which, by the ringing the changes in their collections of bells, churches and cathedrals would sound out a sonic terrain that no one within the acoustic radius of their villages, towns or cities could miss.

It's no surprise that one of the first counties to develop the overwhelmingly English tradition of bell ringing was Lincolnshire. The flat bounds of that eastern county, a place where sea and sky and land melt into one another, create an intimidatingly featureless landscape, especially on a day when the North Sea mist rolls in. But thanks to church bells, you could navigate not through sight, but through sound, by hearing the different peals that bell towers made and working out which you could hear more clearly. You could geo-locate yourself through their sounds, if you were on a pilgrimage to the top of Lincolnshire's most significant hill, where one of its biggest peals of bells rings out from the top of Lincoln Cathedral.

But as well as creating a sonic map in the individual make-up of peals of bells from place to place – the sound of musical time turned into geographic space – the gigantic pieces of music that British church bells create in their nearly endless permutations do something else on a still grander scale: they chart a terrain of mathematical music-making that's a sounding geometry of the spirit. If you have a peal of six bells, the total number of permutations in which they can be rung is 720; if you have eight, it's 40,320; the exponential answer to how many combinations 12 bells gives you is nearly half a billion. That would mean a non-repeating sequence of bell ringing that would last 30 years. No one's ever got close to that mind-boggling feat, but human teams of ringers have managed a record 18 hours without stopping, pealing all the permutations of the eight bells of a church in Loughborough in 1963.

Bells have always sounded the veils of existence: bells to wake the living, bells to raise the dead, bells to sound celebration or communicate alarm, emergency and threat. They have a chameleon-like symbolism for human beings all over the world, from the earliest bells in the historical record, dating from the third millennium BC in China, to the gigantic bells used in Buddhist worship all over South-East Asia, to the biggest bell that has ever existed, the Great Bell of Dhammazedi, lost to the rivers of Burma when the Portuguese stole it in 1608, which weighed over 300 tonnes.

And that complexity and richness of function is implicit in the mystery of the sounds they make. More than any other instrument, bells prove the essential truth that no sound made on an acoustic instrument plays just one frequency, even if you might imagine that's the case when you're playing a single note on a piano, a recorder or a ukulele. In fact, the difference between the same note played on those instruments or any instruments is caused by the different overtones and undertones around the dominant pitch; that particular sonic cocktail of harmonics is how we perceive texture and timbre, and hear one instrument as distinct from another. In most instruments, the dominant pitch sounds the clearest, but, in a bell, that dominant pitch swirls in the middle of a soup of overtones and undertones that resound in a continuous halo. Bells can be tuned more or less precisely, but their richness lies in that halo of harmonics that shrouds every note, every time they are struck. Every bell is a cosmos of musical dimensions, resounding at the same time.

And it's these wondrous musical physics that mean that bells are our passport across veils of life, that they are there at our beginnings and our ends. Or, as the tenor bell – the largest and deepest of any peal – at Winchester Cathedral has inscribed upon it: 'Horas Avolantes Numero, Mortuos Plango: Vivos ad Preces Voco' ('I count the fleeing hours, I lament the dead: the living I call to prayer'), a motto that the composer Jonathan Harvey turned into the title of his piece, Mortuos Plango, Vivos Voco in 1980. In Harvey's music, electronically manipulated recordings of the bell are fused with the voice of his son, who was then a chorister at the cathedral. Harvey's piece is a sonic and spiritual exploration of the physical and symbolical resonances of bell sounds, as if you could crawl inside the sound of a single bell and discover a whole world of meaning and feeling.

The vast majority of the ringable church bell peals in the world are in England, nearly seven thousand of them. The titles of the pieces they play, the methods of the changes that teams of bell-ringers get together to perform, are mathematical sequences of patterns that are called things like Plain Bob, Grandsire Caters or Little Bob Maximus. Those winsome titles disguise the depth of sound and feeling that bell-ringers have been creating since the seventeenth century, charting a place where science meets spirit, where sound meets space, where human beings look up in awe and vibrate in sympathy with the sounds they are making. That's the miraculous logic of bell ringing: *Tintinnalogia* indeed.

PIECE #18

HENRY PURCELL (1659–1695)

DIDO AND AENEAS

London, 1680s

Henry Purcell was a composer of the theatre. His music in London at the end of the seventeenth century made up the sounds of dozens of plays and masques and entertainments for the public theatre and courtly entertainment. His songs for shows like *King Arthur*, *Abdelazar*, and *The Fairy Queen*, his remaking of Shakespeare's *A Midsummer Night's Dream*, were a soundtrack of innovation and imagination for a country and a culture. And what those original audiences heard was Purcell's cosmopolitan consolidation of styles from Italy, France and Germany, a brew of influences that's the secret to what posterity has misconstrued as his monolithically British or English musical achievement. Purcell was a musical internationalist, not a parochial nativist.

And yet Purcell's only opera in the modern terms we understand it – sung all the way through, with the music doing the work of progressing the drama – is one of his shortest theatrical collaborations, and it contains one of the least original but most powerful pieces of music that has been constantly interpreted and reinterpreted by singers, directors, filmmakers and artists across all media ever since the piece was rediscovered at the end of the nineteenth century: *Dido and Aeneas* is the opera, and 'Dido's Lament', the penultimate musical action of the piece, its iconic song.

Part of the contemporary appeal of *Dido and Aeneas* is that it's a whole opera that's only an hour long, yet its three acts are as satisfyingly complete as any longer music-drama. With its directness of plot, its richness of character, and its relatively small demands on its performers, as well as the economy of staging that it requires, *Dido and Aeneas* is a better fit for today's musical culture than the gigantism of Purcell's later so-called 'semi-operas', which were the summit of his theatrical ambition in his lifetime. Pieces like *The Fairy Queen* require musicians, singers, actors, dancers and a staging of sumptuous imagination to be properly realised. *Dido and Aeneas*, by contrast, was performed at Josias Priest's girls' school by its pupils in 1689, when Purcell was no older than 30.

And it was thought for centuries that the opera was composed especially for the school and its pupils, but it's more likely that *Dido and Aeneas* was conceived as a courtly entertainment for Charles II earlier in the 1680s, not least because the story and its musical execution – including the lamenting solo and chorus that the opera ends with – are strikingly similar to his teacher John Blow's hour-long opera *Venus and Adonis*, created in the early 1680s for the court. Purcell, in his mid-twenties, enjoying royal patronage, living in Westminster, and with a reputation as the pre-eminent prodigy of Britain's musical life, wanted not only to imitate Blow's success, but to show that the pupil could make something that even his teacher couldn't.

Working with his librettist, Nahum Tate, Purcell takes the story of Dido at Carthage and her betrayal by Aeneas and turns it into a drama in which the message is clear: women shouldn't trust young men who flatter them with protestations of love. That's true of Aeneas, and it's true for the boozy sailors at the start of Act 3, who sing how blokes should take their 'nymphs' and 'silence their mourning / With vows of returning / But never intending to visit them more'. These words are set to some of Purcell's most ironically joyful music, finding a register of drunken fun that sends up the cynicism and misogyny of the sailors. And their antics prefigure what Aeneas does to Dido: he's with her for one night, declares love, and then leaves her at the earliest chance he can, using the excuse of having to obey Jove's commands and go and fight for Troy. That's the ruse of the Sorcerers – Tate and Purcell's invention – who plot to overthrow Dido; but Aeneas puts up no real resistance.

Dido, with her pride hurt and her certain knowledge of Aeneas' falseness, dies of shame and grief more than she does of lost love. It's her choice to die at the end of the opera – she calls death 'a welcome guest' – and her words in her final lament aren't about losing Aeneas, who doesn't deserve anything like the sincerity or power of her emotion. Instead they are addressed to her faithful Belinda, and to posterity. The whole text of her song is three lines long: 'When I am laid in earth, may my wrongs create / No trouble in thy breast; / Remember me, but ah! Forget my fate'.

Purcell's music for these words is fundamentally un-original. He roots Dido's song on a descending bass line, which rises only to fall again, and again, creating an Escher-like sense of eternal descent, going deeper and deeper down into a pit of pain. That slithery bassline is a familiar musical figure of mourning, with its five sighing semitones, which composers like Barbara Strozzi and Claudio Monteverdi also used earlier in the same century. The significance of that compositional choice is that Purcell is deliberately rehearsing a well-worn convention in order to amplify the power of communication in this moment of the drama. His performers and audiences would understand instantly what was at stake in this song the moment they heard the unadorned bassline that it starts with, symbolising not only this lament, but a whole repertoire of lamenting music, and that's just the start of the slow minor-key keening it unfolds in three minutes of music. And we understand it today too, because that bassline isn't only shared in classical repertoires of lamenting, it's still used across musical cultures today from the blues to folk traditions, especially in Spain and its diaspora.

Yet what truly is original in Purcell's music is how he intensifies the instrumental accompaniment and the relationship with the solo voice, so the string lines weave their own lines of harmonic dissonance and melodic richness below the voice, as if Dido's stoic acceptance of her fate were influencing and changing their music. The instruments become a weeping veil of mourning that melts into the final music in the opera: a vocal chorus in which the 'dropping wings' of multiple Cupids conjure another labyrinth of endless descent.

'Dido's Lament', like the rest of the opera, was hardly performed for nearly two centuries between 1705 and 1895, before it was staged again in London and Dublin that year. Since then, the opera's popularity has exponentially increased in opera houses and concert halls. But it's as a song on its own terms that 'Dido's Lament' has spread throughout the whole of musical culture, in versions across pop from Jeff Buckley's unbearably spare and fragile performance, to Klaus Nomi's epic theatrics. Annie Lennox sang it during the covid pandemic to sound a mourning for the disappearance of live music and the climate crisis: she called her recording a 'lament for a dying planet'. In all of those and countless other performances, and its familiarity at the top of international charts of the most popular piece of classical music ever composed, 'Dido's Lament' has reclaimed its power of communication of pain, desolation and loss for contemporary audiences. And it expresses all of those feelings with an immediacy that feels biological rather than cultural. You don't need to know the whole opera to understand that this music doesn't just represent pain, it embodies it and exorcises it.

'Dido's Lament' has a shamanic power in our imaginations because it comes from a deeper place than Purcell knew. It carries across time and culture in ways that he couldn't have anticipated before his death at the age of just 36 in 1695, but the music itself already knew something its composer didn't in its prehistory and its prefiguring of the laments of future times. We remember, and do not forget the power of the musical and emotional fate that Purcell released and gave to the world.

PIECE #19

ISABELLA LEONARDA
(1620–1704)

SONATAS, OP. 16

Novara, 1693

The sonatas published by Isabella Leonarda, a 73-year-old nun who had been cloistered since the age of 16 in Novara, are the first purely instrumental music to be printed by a named female composer in the West. But these 12 sonatas aren't a solitary late flowering of compositional brilliance: they're one of around 200 pieces that Isabella Leonarda composed, revealing the richness of the musical community of the convent of Saint Ursula in Novara in Northern Italy, and creating one of the most important repertoires of seventeenth-century music.

Leonarda was the most prolific female composer of the seventeenth century, yet she wasn't only the convent's resident composer. She became St Ursula's most important spiritual, organisational and political leader, rising through all the ranks of responsibility to become *superiora* and, ultimately, *consigliera*. That meant that her time for composition was restricted to the few hours in the day not given over to devotional duty. Instead she gave up 'hours of sleep to write these musical compositions of mine, so as not to be found wanting in the obligations of government'. Leonarda became more energetic the older she was, composing the bulk of her music in the last three decades of her life, from the age of around 50.

She was composing in the context of what could have been a deeply anti-musical environment in the way that the church's power was deployed in Novara. As late as 1591, in a letter from the *vicario generale* of the city, the nuns were forbidden to 'possess or play any kind of instrument except the clavichord or violone da gamba used for the bass [the forerunner of the double bass], not to sing any song, madrigal or motet of secular and worldly things, but only of things ecclesiastical and pious … . It will not be lawful to sing polyphony even in the church, but only plain chant'. (They were clearly suffering from the same censorial delusion about multi-voiced music, and the dangerous delights of musical sensuality, that Palestrina's papal masters were too – but they obviously hadn't got the memo that Palestrina had a big win for polyphony in the wake of the Council of Trent in 1562 – see Piece #12.) The *vicario generale* goes on: 'we command … the abbess that at the end of three days she must remove from the monastery any instrument except the clavichord and the above-mentioned [bass] violini, and any book that deals with vain and useless subjects, both musical and any other sort'.

Isabella Leonarda, mercifully, lived in a convent in which those laws were basically ignored in service of the creation of a musical culture that was rich, participatory, and which inspired her to innovate throughout her life. Among the jewels of Leonarda's work is a setting of a version of the same morality play that Hildegard composed in the twelfth century. In her piece *Quo pergis anima*, Leonarda distils the conflict between the devilishly tempting World, and Anima, the Soul, into a scene for four allegorically dramatic characters, which lasts just a few minutes. Her music is written for the all-female soloists to scale the heights of lyricism and plumb the depths of their vocal ranges, culminating in an ecstatic polyphony for all four voices, including the benighted World, praising the Soul's salvation.

The range and imagination of Leonarda's motets on texts of religious reflection, words she likely wrote herself, is jaw-dropping. In her *Dixit Dominus*, a nine-minute paean of praise composed when she was 78 for four voices and violins, she creates an abundance and expressive radiance from the way the instrumental parts weave around the voices, music that must have been written in one of those ecstatic nights when she took herself away from all that governance and could give in to her muse.

And in her 12 instrumental sonatas, Leonarda gloriously discovered new compositional terrain when she was in her early seventies. These pieces would have had a liturgical function within the abbey's rituals, yet these 'church sonatas' are also where the roots of an independent instrumental music lie: they are the precursors of sonatas and symphonies in their four-section structure, full of dramatic and expressive contrast. The inspiration for these pieces isn't the prayer but the dance, the movement of bodies that sing, that exalt, that rejoice.

Late in her life, Leonarda's instrumental pieces find a radical joy in their spirit of play, in their festive fecundity of invention, straddling worlds of sacred ecstasy and secular pleasure. Isabella Leonarda died at the age of 83 in 1704: her legacy in all of the collections of music she leaves her listeners and performers is a life-lesson of musical and spiritual fulfilment, a flame that can't be cloistered.

PIECE #20

ÉLISABETH JACQUET DE LA GUERRE (1665–1729)

CÉPHALE ET PROCRIS

Paris, 1694

The Palais Royal, Paris, 15 May 1694: the premiere of one of the most hyped operas of recent seasons, composed by one of the favourites of the court – Élisabeth Jacquet de la Guerre. She was someone whose virtuosity had delighted the Sun King, Louis XIV, ever since he heard her as a child prodigy, when she played for him at the age of just five at Versailles. At court, her family connections – she came from a dynasty of instrument makers – gave her prodigious access to the King, but she earned her reputation as a composer, a harpsichordist and teacher, becoming one of the most famous musicians of the time. At the age of 22, she published her *First Book of Pieces for the Harpsichord* – music of poetry, subtlety and fantastical imaginative freedom – and a few years later she had already ascended France's Parnassus of creative genius. The writer and creator of France's hierarchies of artistic greatness, Titon de Tillet, put her on the same level as the composers Marin Marais and Michel de Lalande, just one rung below Jean-Baptiste Lully, whose operas for Louis XIV defined the sound and spectacle of the epoch.

Yet Jacquet de la Guerre was about to do something that no one in the court at Versailles or in the charmed circles of French opera had yet done: put on an opera, as a female composer, in a theatre in which she wouldn't even have been allowed to visit the stalls, where all the men – and all the composers

– usually stood, just behind the musicians in the orchestra. Women were only allowed in the upper balconies and galleries of the theatre. They weren't supposed to be down there in the all-male mosh pit – and they weren't expected to be there as composers or musicians.

Jacquet de la Guerre's opera wasn't her first stage work, but it's the only theatrical piece of hers that survives. And the five acts of *Céphale et Procris* are a nod to the conventions of the Palais Royal and the tastes of its aristocratic audiences. The form of the piece is something that fans of Lully's *tragédies lyriques* would recognise, the subject matter is catastrophically doomed love from Ancient Greek myth, as per Lully's example, and her score builds on his achievements too. In its first act, *Céphale et Procris* is full of sounds and images of pastoral togetherness, contrasting with the pits of hell that open up by the time we reach Act 4, and she even includes a long prologue that allegorically extols the virtue of the King. So far, so conventional.

But Jacquet de la Guerre does much more than pay lip service to these traditions in what was the biggest piece of her career so far, and the most important night of her musical life. Her music for her heroine, Procris, is the golden thread throughout the opera. Procris' aria in Act 2, when she is forced apart from her beloved Céphale to appease the whims of the gods, is a miracle of musical subtlety, in which the music is poised on the edge of pleasure and pain, as minor-key harmonies melt into major-key chords, shards of light that make the despair that surrounds them even more poignant. And in Act 4, Jacquet de la Guerre writes Procris an aria in which she longs for her death, before a rumbling earthquake in orchestral sound and theatrical spectacle takes her to the Underworld. There was a long tradition of barnstorming special effects in Parisian opera to mimic the violence of the natural world – volcanoes, storms, sunrises, and much more – but Jacquet de la Guerre turns what could merely be sonic sensation into vivid dramatic psychology. Thanks to the intensity of her music, it's Procris' desolation that opens the gates of the Underworld, not a capriciously theatrical force of nature.

The end of the opera is even more shattering: Céphale has mortally injured Procris by accident at the very moment when there was a prospect of them being together again. Jacquet de la Guerre makes this final scene a shatteringly intimate revelation for the two lovers brought to the end of their lives, giving them music of fragile lyricism with gossamer sighs of accompaniment. Jacquet de la Guerre risks a shocking psychological realism that turns the drama inwards to the souls of the lovers who die for each other. That was a consciously radical choice, eschewing the chorus of corporate conclusion that audiences had grown to expect that every opera at the Palais Royal should end with. Instead, Jacquet de la Guerre invites her audience to share the lovers' tragedy in as raw and desolate way as possible, leaving them with their breaths taken in anguish.

Despite this expressive adventure, *Céphale et Procris* was not a success, closing after just a few performances. Why? Because of cabals who took against the pre-show hype for a composer who was part of the Versaille establishment; because audiences wanted – even then – to see what they knew they liked in revivals of Lully's operas rather than coming to terms with a new drama; and because of the innate patriarchal prejudice against a composer whose very celebrity, and the fact that she was the first woman in France to have a full-scale opera on stage, counted against her. Jacquet de la Guerre retreated from the opera stage, composing innovative chamber music in the first decade of the eighteenth century for violin and harpsichord. But *Céphale et Procris* is her grandest achievement, and it's a piece of her time, and of ours, cutting through convention to find a vivid dramatic and emotional realism. Get it back on our opera stages!

PIECE #21

ROQUE JACINTO DE CHAVARRÍA (1688–1719)

'FUERA, FUERA! HÁGANLES LUGAR!'

The Chiquitos and Moxos musicians of Bolivia, early eighteenth century

The conquest wasn't only about money, power, dominion, empire and subjugation: the Spanish brought with them musical missionaries as part of their colonial project in South America. And by the end of the seventeenth century, the Jesuits in Bolivia worked with local musicians from the Moxos and Chiquitos peoples to create one of the most remarkable eras of musical history.

The Jesuits knew how music could do much of the work of their mission for them: instead of forcing scripture on the peoples of Bolivia, after they had established the infrastructure of the so-called *reducións* (literally, 'reductions'), the physical bases for their mission, they founded choirs and orchestras with the local communities. They knew that music-making was the most effective way to spread the word of the Catholic Church through the embodied experience and participation of the peoples of Bolivia. Singing in their own languages, playing European instruments alongside their own, the Jesuits encouraged the Bolivians to lead their own musical culture: the Chapel Master of these ensembles was a member of the local community, leading by example and encouraging all of the people of the *reducción* to be part of these new forms of worship and music-making.

The Jesuits' mission – until they were removed from South America by King Charles III in 1767 – was superficially more benign than other forms of military and cultural conquest, since it didn't seek an erasure of Bolivian music, but an incorporation of native languages, instruments and musical forms into a new repertoire. Yet the project was clear: the transformation of the holders of native religious traditions into adherents of Catholic dogma. Music's soft power in embodying this new religious community in action is no less a part of the essential power dynamics of colonialism, for all the richness of the repertoire it produced.

But the surviving repertoires in Bolivia also reveal something else: this music is a two-way dialogue, in the influence of Bolivian cultures on the European Baroque styles in the pieces composed, created and copied by anonymous Chiquitos and Moxos musicians. It's a record of a distinct tradition of music-making that could only happen because of the ownership and participation of the Bolivian peoples, returning the colonial gaze back on the music that the Jesuits arrived with: not an eradication of native traditions, but a conversation across continents and cultures. That means a meeting of the notated instrumental music, for strings, keyboards and winds, of the seventeenth century that the Jesuits brought with them, along with their ecclesiastical vocal repertoire, mixing with the initially oral traditions of the peoples of Bolivia, and their own instruments.

Yet not all the sources of this music are anonymous. The composer Roque Jacinto de Chavarría was born in La Plata, now Sucre, in Bolivia in 1688 to mixed heritage parents. His mother died in 1695, and he was taken in by the cathedral's community, becoming one of its musicians and composers. He died at the age of just 32 in 1719, but among the handful of pieces he leaves to the world is a miniature choral *scena*, '*Fuera, fuera! Háganles lugar!*' ('Get away from here! Make space!'), which is staged as a dialogue between the 'Spaniards' and the 'Indians' at Christ's nativity. And in music that teems with a rhythmic energy that's full of de Chavarría's Bolivian interpretation of the cross-rhythms and syncopations of European music, which he takes to an irresistible extreme, he dramatises an encounter between the Spaniards who tell everyone to 'get away' from the remote tribe of Indians, who are 'noisily going to breathe on he who is in the stable'. The Indians reply: 'Do not mock us, Spanish shepherd, all of us are simply people who are sons of Adam', and after the music's call-and-response style exchanges, de Chavarría distils this colonial confrontation to a final musical image of the Indians and Spaniards singing together in praise of the Christ-child.

The sounds of this piece are the sounds of this unique meeting of cultures in action: the way the voices chase one another across the bar-lines, the way the 'Indians' assert their own identity and do not capitulate to the Spaniards, and instead it's the Spaniards who are convinced by their argument that every person is a son of Adam, and that they all have a right to be there at the manger. The evidence of the cultural erasures of conquest and colonialism are everywhere in South America. But in vivid fragments like de Chavarría's piece, another story emerges, of a Bolivian composer taking on the European gaze and returning it, with piquancy, challenge and energy: as the indigenous Quecha word in the lyrics says: '*Achalay, achalay!*' – 'Rejoice, rejoice!'.

PIECE #22
THE C MAJOR SCALE

The C major scale – the white notes of the piano, the sound of major modality, eight notes from one C to another an octave higher: it's the ur-piece, the first complete phrase that millions of keyboard players all over the world will ever play. What could be simpler?

In fact, the reason the C major scale sounds the way it does hides a history of centuries of debate, philosophy, and the technique of tuning in Western music.

Let's go back from the major scale to the semitones that lie behind it, the totality of the white and black keys between one C and another on the keyboard. There's no necessary reason that distance should be the 12 equal semitones that the vast majority of keyboards are now tuned to. (The semitone is the smallest interval on the piano keyboard, the difference between a black key and the white notes either side of it.) Other ways of tuning are available and are used in the musics of Indonesia, South-East Asia, Japan, India and many other cultures: more notes, or fewer, to split the octave, tuning systems that are richer and more complex and nuanced in sound and feeling than those 12 equal steps of the piano.

The reason that pianos have the notes they do is that the 12 semitones are an approximation of the overtones of the harmonic series, the secret resonances behind any note that you hear played on an acoustic instrument. Take any C on the piano: what you hear as a single note is actually made up of a constellation of vibrating notes, above and beneath the dominant note you perceive as that C. The relative strength of the different frequencies in that halo of tones accounts for why we hear instrumental colours the way we do. That's true of bells (see Piece #17), that's true of pianos, and it's true of any instrument; the differences between the make-up of that swirl of harmonics is what makes us hear the acoustic distinction between the same pitch when it's played on the clarinet or the horn, the cello or the piano.

And those harmonics are vibrating in frequencies that aren't in tune with the compromises of the way that most pianos are tuned all over the world in the relationship between the pitch of one note and the next. That's thanks to the system of so-called 'equal temperament' which began to take over Western music in the nineteenth century, and is now the most dominant way of hearing and creating music across the globe. The ratios between those 12 semitones, the idea that they should be as similar, as 'equal' as possible, are embedded not only in the way piano strings are tuned, but the software of sequencer programmes, and in the vast majority of music that's produced commercially anywhere in the world. For billions of us human beings, the sound of music is equally tempered, and is surely supposed to be.

But that's not true. To hear what naturally tempered scales sound like, in tune with the harmonics that shimmer around each note as they really are, and not as Western pianos would like them to be, you need to experience repertoires like the classical musics of India, which are built on tuning into the resonances around a single fundamental pitch. The choice that Indian cultures make is to build whole performances on those drones, and fly into the stratosphere of all the notes that are sounding in the halo of that fundamental pitch, to be both grounded by the drone and to use it as inspiration for musical freedom.

Western musical cultures are made of a different principle, which is the idea that music can move from one fundamental tone to another, that it can modulate from one key to another: from, say, C major, to G major, to F major and back to C again. But if you're going to move from one musical place to another, you have to have the possibility that the same tune will sound equally well with a new fundamental tone as it did before. And to do that, you need to compromise the natural harmonics and their halo of resonances; you need to stretch and compress them so that they fit the 12 equally spaced semitones of the piano.

That compromise is the canker in the apple of Western music, and it has a name: the Pythagorean comma, after one of the world's foremost mathematicians and musical theorists in Greece in the sixth century BC. Pythagoras realised that you have a choice: you can either have your fifths or your octaves in tune – but you can't have both. If you keep extrapolating your fifths out in a cycle from one note, you have to jump 12 steps to get back to where you started, cycling through all 12 of the pitches of the chromatic scale, starting at C and ending up back at C again. But here's the kicker: if you do that with 'natural' fifths, tuned in sympathy with the true resonances of the harmonic series, you'll actually be out of tune with your fundamental note by the time you get the whole way round, so that your two Cs will sound shimmeringly out of sync. The 'comma' is the distance of that out-of-tuneness.

It's a beautiful – and paradoxical – phenomenon of acoustics, and it's the piquancy of the choice that Western music has made that inspires the richness of its repertoires, the way it can create a feeling of movement from one key-centre to another, and how it can give us those spine-tingling changes of harmonies in your favourite song.

But it also means that the way that Western and Western-inspired music sounds is a compromise between nature and culture. So to bring us back to C: don't take the C major scale for granted – there are whole universes of sound right there under your fingertips, in the secret stories and the spectra of sound that teem behind every note you play.

PIECE #23

JOHANN PACHELBEL (1653–1706)

CANON IN D MAJOR

Germany, before 1706

Not so much a piece of music as an industry: Johann Pachelbel's Canon in D major – really, the first part of a canon and gigue – is one of music's most notoriously popular pieces of classical music, which has spread through musical culture like a bountiful blooming, for its fans, and a form of virulent musical knotweed, for those who have heard it too many times on the end of calls where you're reassured that 'your business is important to us', but the only proof is a canned recording of Pachelbel's Canon on a seemingly eternal loop, a performance over your phone speaker that succumbs to the same mania of repetition that the piece itself is all about, but which only succeeds in implanting the music in your brain for another day, locking you yet again in a Pachelbel-prison from which it seems there's no escape …

But don't worry, it's only a piece of music. And a short one, at that, whose circumstances of composition are unknown. (There's a rumour that it was composed for the wedding of Johann Christoph Bach, Johann Sebastian's brother, in 1694, but it's – alas! – a story too good to be true, that the world's most popular piece for wedding playlists was itself written for a composer's nuptials.) There is no manuscript in Pachelbel's own handwriting, and the piece is only known from a later copy, from the mid-eighteenth century. The Canon is only a few minutes long, just 56 bars on the page, in which the bass part plays exactly the same 8 notes precisely 28 times, over and over. There is effectively only one line of music above it, it's just that the three violins – or whichever arrangement you're hearing at the wedding, funeral, or stately civic event you're attending – are playing the same music at slightly different times, two bars apart.

That all means that Pachelbel's Canon isn't only its own musical industry – albeit one from which its composer never made any meaningful money: imagine the royalties that Pachelbel ought to have been paid! – it's literally a musical machine, made of a precise interlocking of parts in its exquisitely sophisticated round. That's what a 'canon' is: like any playground round (think of 'Row, row, row your boat'), one person starts a melody, then another joins a few moments later, and then another, and the song is only finished when everyone has got through the tune.

The dues that Pachelbel should have been paid on his Canon – hundreds of millions of pounds, if copyright laws never expired – come from all corners of musical culture from the twentieth century onwards, when the piece was rediscovered. In recordings from the 1960s and 1970s, Pachelbel's Canon went to the top of the classical charts, and was listeners' most requested track on radio stations all over the world. It also fired the imagination of pop composers and producers, who turned the Pachelbel progression, the harmonies suggested by those first eight notes of the bass line, into a musical shorthand that underpins hits from Procol Harum to Kylie Minogue.

So why has this particular musical machine been so infernally popular, to the total exclusion of all the other music that Pachelbel composed, the volumes of chamber music and instrumental variations, that made him such an important composer, organist and teacher in Germany and Austria in the late seventeenth century, before his death in 1706?

It's because the piece is all about relishing a dance between predictability and unpredictability. That safely, squarely repeated bass line is enriched not only by the voices that come in one by one above it, but by our listening: our imaginations unconsciously fill in the implications of the relationship between the bass and the first voice, and the second, and the third. And then we're surprised and delighted when Pachelbel thrills us with a new variation, when the first violin starts dancing with super-quick demisemiquavers, a joy you realise you can experience again and again, when the other violins play the same music in the Canon's endless chain of musical time of the piece.

Pachelbel's Canon is a piece of music that feels as physically satisfying as a string of pearls in your hands, because its form allows you to hear the music in three dimensions. It's made of a tessellation of those three violins, playing the same music, one after the other, and by the harmonies that result from how they stack up on top of one another. The Canon expresses a perfect little symmetry of horizontal, melodic time and vertical, chordal instantaneity. Your listening adds still another dimension, as you try and predict what's coming next, bouncing off the reliable repetitions of the bassline.

It's not just for weddings, and it's not only fodder for pop hits: it's that always reassuring yet always surprising variety that makes this Canon of all canons so popular. Pachelbel's Canon is an infinitely pleasurable listening machine, as long as you want it to be – and so long as your call is finally answered.

PIECE #24

JOHANN SEBASTIAN BACH
(1685–1750)

ST MATTHEW
PASSION

Leipzig, 1727–1729

The status of what constitutes a 'piece of music' is central to this book: I have the image of a flame being passed down, still burning brightly, after however many centuries separate the original composition and creation from our time. In Johann Sebastian Bach's case, the *St Matthew Passion* was his piece of pieces. He lavished more care and attention on his manuscript copy of this Passion than on any of his other works; writing it out in inks of different colours, so that the biblical words of the Evangelist, the solo tenor part, are notated in a deep red, as are all of the texts that come from the Gospel, contrasting with the black for the rest of the manuscript, the music for the double orchestra, double choir and soloists.

Bach repaired this vast score after it was damaged, painstakingly writing out the music again, binding and sewing the score, drawing all of its staves and barlines by hand, leaving this document as the most precious and sacred of all his possessions. At the time he was making revisions and repairs to this manuscript, late in his life, Bach's music was profoundly out of fashion, because of its scale and complexity, its rhetorical richness and devotional symbolism. The world would have to catch up, decades and centuries later, to his achievement in the *St Matthew Passion*. Bach's lifelong preservation and care for this score, more than any of the more than one thousand he composed in his lifetime – and more than his scores for his *St*

John Passion, and his lost *St Mark Passion* – is an act of faith in the future as great as his Lutheran religious devotion to the Resurrection and the afterlife. Bach wanted this manuscript to last, to be a hard-won jewel of faithfulness thrown into an unknown future, a promise to be redeemed by unborn generations in their performances.

And redeemed it has been, in countless interpretations ever since Felix Mendelssohn conducted an edited performance of the piece in Leipzig in 1829. That's the moment when the *St Matthew Passion* emerged into the public consciousness again, after decades of silence. Even at that distance from its composition, the Passion was considered unperformable as a totality, despite the clarity of Bach's score, despite the will and testament of his intentions for this piece in that stunning manuscript.

Every act of interpretation of the *St Matthew Passion* ever since, in churches, in concert halls, and in theatrical stagings – like the unforgettable concert hall dramatisation of the piece that Peter Sellars directed with the Berlin Philharmonic, conducted by Simon Rattle in 2010, in which every person in the audience was turned into a participant – is a unique journey through the immense labyrinth of Bach's composition. There is no definitive *St Matthew Passion* in performance; its spiritual richness, its multi-dimensional complexity in the way its texts and idioms and voices are layered on top of one another means that its entire range, let alone its meaning, cannot be contained or revealed in any single interpretation. And yet the monument of the piece itself, Bach's act of preservation in his lifetime in his manuscript, is unquestionably, solidly there: the still point around which every performance, every audience interaction, swirls in a constant state of energy: a motion towards the piece, and an intertwining with it.

This unfinishable chain of interpretation comes from the fact that the *St Matthew Passion* is really a collection of pieces, modes of communication, and invitations to participate in it. That's most obvious in the fact that it consists of no fewer than 68 numbers, from the first chorus to the last, and there are so many different types of musical action contained with its spiritual dramaturgy. The Evangelist is the tenor soloist who narrates the words of the Gospel and leads us through the progress of the story. The character of Jesus is sung by a solo bass, who is almost always surrounded by a halo of strings when he sings – apart from during his final appearance, for his despairing words from the cross: 'My God, my God, why hast thou forsaken me?'. The arias, for solo voices, and with interventions from the chorus, set apocryphal texts that reflect on the journey towards Jesus' death, the moment in the biblical drama where the piece ends. And it's the chorus who take on the greatest variety of roles in the piece, baying for Jesus' blood, praying for his salvation, and connecting their congregation of voices with ours in the huge choral fantasias they sing, at the very beginning of the Passion, the conclusion of the first part, and in its final number.

And in the chorales, the hymns. The chorales that stud the *St Matthew Passion* are among the most moving pieces of music ever collaboratively composed and performed. The tunes aren't Bach's: they come from the repertoire of Lutheran hymn tunes that were part of the fabric of congregational life at St Thomas' Church in Leipzig where Bach was working. They are moments in which the real-life congregation of the audience in the church are enlisted as part of the spiritual work of this piece. They are expressions of a visceral connection between Bach and his listeners, who are addressed as participants, not mere witnesses, in the drama of the Passion. The congregation would have sung these chorales along with the chorus of performers, collapsing the usual difference between them and us in most classical music settings: everyone in a performance of the *St Matthew Passion* should be involved.

Bach uses 10 chorale tunes, and re-harmonises them as they are repeated throughout the piece. They function like a knife through the canvas of the piece, dissolving aesthetic distance in an instant, pointing the action squarely at the souls of every individual listener. Soaked in imagery of blood, sacrifice and martyrdom, the chorales force the drama into the present tense of the performance. The chorales say to all of us: we are all part of this drama. They put us at the heart of the story, next to Jesus, in Jerusalem, in Gethsemane, at Golgotha.

Bach's intensification of the dissonance in his harmonisations of the '*O Haupt voll Blut und Wunden*' ('O Sacred Head Now Wounded') chorale, the most-used tune in the piece with its five appearances, is one of the most obvious threads of crimson experience with which the Passion becomes progressively drenched. The tune doesn't change, but the feelings it inspires become progressively more painful in Bach's harmonisations underneath it, until it's as if the music itself has become saturated by Christ's open wounds. Its final appearance, after the crucifixion, is among the most agonising moments ever conceived in music in the chains of dissonance that Bach composes, and makes us feel. Bach forces us not to look away, but to be there with the sacrifice, next to the blood, burning with astonishment at the Passion.

And that's just one of the dimensions of musical and spiritual time that the *St Matthew Passion* opens up. The three massive choruses that open, close, and divide the piece aren't monolithic blocks, they're made of music that's designed to physically fly across the space of the performance in the relationship between the two orchestras and multiple choirs, all occupying different parts of the performance space, in a church or in a concert hall. These huge choral pieces each have different scales of musical motion which are matched by their wildly different emotional terrain: there's the restless searching of the opening chorus, the breathtaking but fragile entreaty of the chorus at the end of Part 1, and the traumatised longing for peace of the very final number.

Throughout the piece, Bach writes music that shifts between all of its modes of dramatisation in an instant – between choruses, arias, and the Evangelist's increasingly emotional, involved narration – making a tapestry of time that insists above all on the urgency of the present tense. Christ's Passion becomes our passion, our story and our responsibility, whatever our faith, whatever our historical epoch. When you're listening to the Passion, you are folded into its infinite moment.

The reason that Bach's *St Matthew Passion* is his piece of pieces is that, in caring so deeply for the single artefact of his manuscript, Bach offers us an eternity of responses in our interpretations, performances and auditions of the music. The Passion is a piece whose resonances, meanings and miracles never end.

PIECE #25

GEORGE FRIDERIC HANDEL
(1685–1759)

MESSIAH

Dublin, 1742

Where Bach's *St Matthew Passion* is a journey inwards to the desperate intimacy of the scene beside the cross, Handel's oratorio *Messiah* takes the reverse course: outwards, towards the world, towards joy, social connection and renewal. Handel's *Messiah* is the sound of charity in musical action, in the substance of its music, in the tradition of its performances in Handel's lifetime, and ours.

The roots of its transformation into its own tradition of charity are already there in the circumstances of its first performances in Dublin, and, above all, in the concerts of *Messiah* that were given from 1750 onwards at the Foundling Hospital in London, Thomas Corum's school for orphaned children. These children would otherwise have been cast out of society, stigmatised for being illegitimate, and victims of the social prejudices that so often broke the hearts and souls of the women who bore them and who had to give them up. The Foundling Hospital museum today shows a collection of tokens given by the mothers of the children who would use them to reclaim their families if their circumstances changed. Today, these physical emblems of maternal love given as unclaimed promises bring the social injustices of an age immediately to life, when you hold a thimble, a child's ring, a coin split in two, or a hazelnut in your hand, each representing the bond of a mother with her child that could not be redeemed.

Yet the sounds of Handel's *Messiah* are a transcendence of those times too. Handel wrote the piece with typical speed – it took him just over three weeks in 1741 – an alacrity that was neither negligent, nor did it represent a unique fever of divine inspiration. Handel always had to work this fast to get his new operas or oratorios written in time for the new season in London. He started another major work, *Samson*, just after finishing *Messiah*, and he completed that one in three weeks as well.

But *Messiah* was more than just another job for Handel, who had moved to London from Germany 30 years earlier. He needed it to be successful after the relative commercial failure of his previous oratorio, *Israel in Egypt*. *Messiah* was a piece that Handel kept on believing in, kept revising, and kept reworking for the performances throughout the 1740s.

It took years for *Messiah* to catch on in London, but at its first performances in Dublin, it was a different story: *Messiah* was a sensation in 1742. Two charitable performances were given in April and June, and for the premiere, the beneficiaries were the Mercer's Hospital, the Charitable Infirmary and prisoners' debt relief. No fewer than 142 prisoners were released from debtors' prison as a result of how much money the performance earned.

In Dublin, Handel knew the mezzo-soprano soloist Susanna Cibber especially well, one of his favourite artists. Cibber was an actor and singer who had been publicly shamed in London for the failure of her marriage in the late 1730s; she retired from the London stage and rehabilitated her career in Dublin in the 1741 season. Cibber was the first singer of one of *Messiah*'s unforgettable arias, 'He was despised', in Part 2 of the piece. Handel composes music of deceptively meditative simplicity for the outer sections of this aria, a picture of Christ's dignity in the face of the violence and indifference of the world. Handel vividly describes those horrors in a lashing minor-key central section – 'He hid not His face from shame and spitting', set to music of terrifying vividness – before the opening section returns, now with an even greater radiance and nobility. After Cibber had sung it for the very first time, a Dublin clergyman, Dr. Delany, exclaimed: 'Woman, for this be all thy sins forgiven thee!' Not that Cibber had any real 'sins' to be forgiven; but even in this first performance, *Messiah*'s work of personal as well as charitable transformation had started.

In London, *Messiah* was only intermittently revived as part of subsequent oratorio seasons. But something changed in 1750, when Handel performed *Messiah* as a benefit concert at The Foundling Hospital. He was invited to become a Governor after the success of the performance; these became annual concerts of *Messiah* that Handel directed until his blindness prevented him from conducting. The vision of *Messiah* as a charitable musical work at The Foundling Hospital – the performances raised £7000, around a million pounds in today's money, in Handel's lifetime – transformed the oratorio's public success. Handel was even there to witness the performance in his last year of life, 1759. Handel knew by then as a radiant certainty that his music released an empathy for the Christ-child and the Passion with a vividness and power that could bind people together. He died eight days after the performance, but the mission of *Messiah* had only just begun.

Messiah's performance history is based on the thrill of voices coming together to make something bigger than themselves, extending into dimensions of sound and feeling that none of us as mere individuals can create. The chorus is the heart of any performance of the piece. It's not the virtuosity of the soloists or the orchestra, it's the chorus who make the drama, the story, and the physical and spiritual immediacy of Handel's music. They are the ones who make his yoke easy, who follow Christ like sheep, who lift up their heads to the King of glory.

And who sing Hallelujah: the Hallelujah chorus, with its trumpets and drums and D major fanfares to herald the reign of the Lord God Omnipotent, stands not just for the essential joyfulness of this piece, but the sound of celebration, secular as much as sacred, mundane as well as spiritual. The British tradition of audiences standing as if to attention during this part of *Messiah* is a misrepresentation of the time that King George II is thought to have jumped up from his seat to honour the music when he heard it, meaning that the rest of the audience would have had to follow him. The tradition cannot have started there, since George didn't actually attend the performance where this idea supposedly took hold: instead of royal summons, it's better to think of this moment as a spontaneous standing ovation that the audiences of the 1750s could not resist creating, standing to give collective thanks to Handel, to stand with the chorus, to be part of their project to sing for a whole community.

Most choruses who sing *Messiah* are amateurs, there for the love of music and of communality – and of money: not their own, but to raise funds at performances at Christmas or Easter, for charities in their countries and communities. The annual massed *Messiah*s at the Royal Albert Hall in London turn the entire audience into singers in a non-rehearsed performance that raises the roof – and tens of thousands of pounds.

And the same charitable energy of *Messiah* is there all over the world, in performances from America to Japan: no piece of music in history has raised as much money for charity as *Messiah* has over the centuries. That's a continuation of the purpose that's there in *Messiah*'s origins, in the generosity of Handel's music, and its openness to new interpretations for every time and place of its performance, from Mozart's reorchestration of it in the 1780s to the Gospel *Messiah* that the conductor Marin Alsop curated in the twenty-first century. Handel's *Messiah* radiates the principle of community and charity in action. Its work is always necessary, and forever relevant.

PIECE #26

JOSEPH BOLOGNE, CHEVALIER DE SAINT-GEORGES (1745–1799)

L'AMANT ANONYME

Paris, 1780

Only one of Bologne's operas survives complete: just one of the six that the composer, violinist, fencer and soldier Joseph Bologne composed in one of the most astonishing lives in eighteenth-century history. His operas were the main pieces that he devoted his compositional maturity to in Paris, yet Bologne was the victim in his lifetime – and for too many decades and centuries after his death – of institutional prejudice and racism. He was born in Haiti in 1745, the son of the plantation owner Georges Bologne de Saint-Georges, whose mother, known as Nanon, was one of Georges's wife's slaves. Bologne travelled to France with his father to be educated as the son of an aristocrat, but if Joseph had been born female, no such privileges would have been given, and he would have stayed in Haiti as an illegitimate child of colonial sexual oppression.

But in France, Joseph made himself one of the most famously talented all-rounders in all fields of eighteenth-century life that Paris, and the whole of revolutionary Europe, ever saw. He won a fencing competition in front of Louis XVI, and as a violinist he rose through the ranks of one of the city's most brilliant instrumental ensembles, Le Concert des Amateurs, becoming its director before he turned 30. He was stopped from leading the Paris Opera because of a racist cabal who wouldn't have a person of colour leading them, but at the Concert de la Loge Olympique, the most prestigious and famous concert-giving orchestra in Europe in the 1780s, he commissioned and directed Joseph Haydn's Paris Symphonies, before giving himself to composing operas for the rest of the decade. And he did all of that as well as becoming one of the most decorated soldiers of the revolution, a captain and colonel of the world's first citizen's army, and the leader of the first brigade of non-white soldiers in Europe.

But Bologne's revolutionary ideals weren't only expressed on the battlefield: his music puts egalitarianism centre-stage in the fabric of its sounds and structures. Bologne's instrumental and orchestral music, especially his concertos, is all about a generosity of material that's shared across its soloists and orchestral players. Bologne's *symphonies concertantes* take the principle even further, developing the earlier forms of the Baroque *concerto grosso* into music for multiple soloists whose virtuosity is one of musical empathy, as much as the fantastic and stratospheric technical demands he asks of his soloists. His opus ten pieces, concertos for two violins and viola, were heard by the young Mozart, who loved some of their most bravura gestures, especially the way the soloists chase each other up and up their instruments, thrillingly and vertiginously. Mozart stole and rewrote that idea in the finale of his own Sinfonia Concertante: Bologne is the originator, Mozart the imitator.

And in his opera *L'amant anonyme*, Bologne puts his ideal community on the operatic stage. *The Anonymous Lover* is about the love between Léontine and Valcour. It's Valcour who is the 'anonymous lover' all along, hiding in plain sight, unable to communicate his emotions until the end of the opera. The show ends with two couples from different ends of the social spectrum, servants and masters and mistresses, getting together in a double wedding: a happy ending that Bologne celebrates with a final tableau of instrumental music, a *contredanse*. That's partly in fulfilment of the dances that Parisian audiences loved in their operas, but it's a subversively communitarian gesture as well. In the *contredanse*, there are no divisions between social strata, in the way the dancers move and intertwine with one another. Knowing the hypocrisy of aristocratic prejudice first hand, Joseph Bologne puts his vision of a society that comes together across social divides on stage: the music is decorous, gentle, content, but the compositional intent is radical and political.

Bologne's ability to find music for all five principals of the opera, and have them express confusion, doubt, love and faith, all at the same time, is one of the miracles of the score. That's especially true in the final number of the first act: Valcour has revealed himself to be the anonymous lover who's sending Léontine bouquets – but in a fit of embarrassment, he then pretends it's all a joke. Bologne finds a responsiveness and quicksilver energy that realises this emotional confusion, from the feverish figurations in the strings to the harmonic suspensions that ache in sympathy with the characters' multiple motivations. In music like this, *L'amant anonyme* shows exactly why Bologne knew his operas were his most ambitious and resonant achievement.

Yet Bologne's life and reputation were betrayed many times over in the new century, after his death in 1799. The first betrayal was from the revolution to which he gave his music and his life, since Napoleon reintroduced slavery in 1802, making France the only country on earth to legalise slavery after having banned it, erasing Bologne's music because of his heritage. The next was the loss of most of the musical material of his five other operas, to be followed by the blindness, conservatism and prejudice of Western history and its institutions, which failed to recognise the importance of his music, and his life. *L'amant anonyme* is a revelation, and a piece that the twenty-first century has belatedly started to reclaim. Bologne's real legacy has just begun as his pieces return to concert halls and opera houses – at long last.

PIECE #27

WOLFGANG AMADÉ MOZART
(1756–1791)

THE MARRIAGE
OF FIGARO

Vienna, 1786

The *Marriage of Figaro*, the play by Pierre Beaumarchais, premiered in Paris in 1784, and was personally banned in Vienna by the Emperor, Joseph II: 'since the play contains much that is objectionable, I therefore expect that the Censor shall either reject it altogether, or at any rate have such alterations made in it that he shall be responsible for the performance of this play and for the impression it may make'. The elements deemed 'objectionable' are easy to understand from the perspective of a relatively benign but nonetheless despotic imperial ruler, as Joseph II was, in the 1780s. Nowhere on the continent was immune to the emerging philosophy and ideals of Enlightenment thinking. The turning of philosophy and reason into principled action, such that 'all people shall be brothers', as Friedrich Schiller had written in his 'Ode to Joy' in 1785, was a clear and present danger for Joseph II in Vienna just as much as it was for the royals in Paris, who were sitting on a powder keg of revolution, which would explode in 1789. Beaumarchais's play, under the skin of the comedic and farcical interplay of its characters on a single day at a castle in Seville, shows how the servant classes – embodied by Figaro and Susanna – can plot against their aristocratic overlords, and that it's they, not the abusive, rapacious Count Almaviva, who will have the last laugh.

The play is all about overturning the *droit de seigneur*, the tradition by which aristocrats could sexually abuse their servants on their wedding night, treating them as unwilling concubines. From our perspective, what's most truly 'objectionable' in the play is how the Count tries all he can to hang on to this supposed right because of his desire to possess Susanna. The example the Count gives Cherubino, the teenager who is in love with the Countess and in lust with every woman in the story, is an object lesson in how to get away with it, so that Cherubino has become an abuser in training by the end of the story – what could be more objectionable than that? But that wasn't Joseph II's beef with the story: instead it was the sedition and cleverness of the servants over their masters, above all Susanna's sharpness and emotional intelligence. A servant – and a woman – pulling the strings of her master, seeing him for what he is, and showing him up to the world. This simply couldn't be allowed in Vienna!

And yet Mozart's librettist, Lorenzo da Ponte, managed a miracle, in one of the most brilliant pieces of cultural politicking in European history. While the play was banned in Vienna, da Ponte's adaptation of Beaumarchais's play as a drama for music was allowed to be produced. Da Ponte didn't soften the essential facts of what happens in the story, but he allowed enough gaps for Mozart's music to do the talking, so that the censors were placated, and on 1 May 1786 at the Burgtheater, *Le nozze di Figaro* (the imperial opera was an Italian-language institution in Vienna) was premiered, with Mozart himself leading the performances from the keyboard. So many of the numbers were encored that posters had to be put up – written by the Emperor himself – saying that nothing would be repeated in future performances apart from solo arias, otherwise the shows would be too long.

In its initial run of nine performances, *Figaro* was a success. Joseph II even requested a private performance, and when it was performed later in Prague, *Figaro* made Mozart's operatic reputation. Everyone on the streets, he said, whistles tunes from *Figaro* – and the city commissioned his next collaboration with da Ponte, *Don Giovanni*.

The music in *The Marriage of Figaro* acts as a social leveller, insisting on the humanity of all of the characters in the story, not making their social class their defining characteristic. And Mozart's score clarifies the intentions of every person on stage so sharply that even when they are singing together, they can be expressing completely different points of view, and utterly opposite emotional reactions, but it's all miraculously comprehensible to the audience. Mozart allows that whole range of human comedy to exist simultaneously.

That's what happens in the finale of the second act, when Mozart composes the longest single span of continuous music of his entire life: 20 minutes and more, in which the scene grows from a duet to a trio, from a quartet to a frenetic ensemble of seven characters on stage. The engine of the drama is Mozart's compassion for all of the characters in his score, whether it's Susanna and the Countess plotting to reveal the Count's infidelity, or Figaro putting a spanner in the works of their best-laid plans by saying he was the one who jumped out the window, ruining the flowers below. The music plunges breathtakingly from one style to another, from one escalation of speed to a still higher state of delirium, so you feel you're on a tightrope of musical drama. But in the middle of all this energy, Mozart pulls back the curtain to make a musical revelation in C major, setting words in which the Countess and Susanna ask for the

Count's compassion. The orchestra suddenly creates a slow, pastoral hymn, a still point of the spinning drama all around it.

At the very end of the opera, the Count's priapism is unmasked, and he begs for forgiveness from the Countess, which she gives him in music of heart-melting sincerity. It all happens in just a few bars of G major radiance, which seems to convince the Countess that the Count is genuine, and the music becomes a prayer that the whole cast sing in an outpouring of loving unity. The individuals on stage become a single super-character in a chorus of forgiveness for each other. It's music that radiates its power to all of us listening, consoling us for the joys and misdemeanours of our own romantic lives, and giving us the possibility of hope.

But the opera doesn't end there: Mozart stages a wild party in D major for the opera's last couple of minutes. So which is the truth? The prayer that says all is forgiveness, radiance and light, or the earthbound party that says instead that it's all going to kick off again tomorrow, and that the Count's cycle of abusing won't stop there, that Cherubino will take his turn next, that a revolution of equality across the classes can't just happen in a single moment of G major balm?

The question is the point of the whole opera: Mozart is too empathetic and too intelligent to think that his opera could only be a manifesto for social action; he's too understanding and lovingly accepting of every dimension of human emotion to think there can be a single answer to any human problem of the heart, of sexuality, of society. That's why *The Marriage of Figaro* is necessary in our time. We see ourselves up there on stage, and we feel the music inside us in the places of resonance that Mozart opens up.

In its countless interpretations and productions, from eigh-teenth-century chocolate box throwbacks to stagings like Netia Jones's for the Paris Opera in 2022, which dared to put the hierarchies of a contemporary opera house on the stage – including its sexual abuses and cycles of violence – to the billions of whistlings of its top tunes that anyone who's heard it carries around with them their whole lives: *Figaro*, a new dimension in music theatre in 1786, is still a mirror for our spirits and our societies today.

PIECE #28

LUDWIG VAN BEETHOVEN
(1770–1827)

SYMPHONY NO. 9

Vienna, 1824

The point isn't the premiere of the Ninth Symphony, although that is a seismic moment in Beethoven's life and in the cultural life of Vienna: 7 May 1824 at the Kärntnertor Theatre, with the 53-year-old Beethoven on stage, supposedly conducting the performance, but in fact following the orchestra and singers, since his deafness meant he couldn't meaningfully participate in the music-making.

Beethoven was conducting the ideal performance he was hearing in his head, while the musicians followed the leaders they could actually trust. It's a performance with its own mythologies of tragedy and triumph, including anecdotal moments when Beethoven, still conducting even the though the musicians had stopped playing in the second movement, was turned around by the solo soprano to see the audience applauding. At the very end of the performance, after the frenzied final minutes of the symphony for the choir, soloists and the orchestra, who had to play and sing faster and more furiously than anyone had ever asked them to do before, the audience all waved handkerchiefs, knowing their hero couldn't hear their acclaim.

Beethoven had put on the concert at his own cost, and the premiere played to a full house – including Vienna's Chancellor, Klemens von Metternich, as well as Beethoven's closest friends and champions, such as the composers Franz

Schubert and Carl Czerny. But at the second performance a couple of weeks later, the hall was not full, even if the playing and singing were better.

Those personal and circumstantial stories are only the first of so many histories in which the Ninth Symphony is enmeshed, and which it has created. The piece's essential challenge to humanity is that its utopian dreams, its setting of Friedrich Schiller's 'Ode To Joy' in its unprecedented finale for choir, and soloists – no symphony had included a choir or voices before – have never been realised in the world outside the concert hall, with its vision of 'all people' embracing together, united by the 'kiss of the whole world'. And, para-doxically, that's exactly why the Ninth Symphony goes on being so necessary, as its ideals and the reality of the world spiral apart ever more exponentially.

And yet, while the symphony as a whole has not properly been turned into human action, the quick fix of the main theme of its finale, the 'Ode to Joy' itself, certainly has. Beethoven's sketches show how long and how hard he worked to find a tune that would be worthy of the ideals of Schiller's words, which he'd written in 1785 and which Beethoven had known and wanted to set for decades. His challenge was to write a melody that would realise the idea of universal brotherhood. He wanted and needed to write nothing less than an anthem for a new world to sing.

Beethoven was inspired by the anthems of the countries and the republics he knew so well, some of which he had already incorporated into previous pieces: Beethoven admired every-thing from 'God Save the King' to 'The Marseillaise' to Haydn's 'Emperor Hymn', the tune we now know as the '*Deutschlandlied*',

Germany's national anthem. Beethoven's tune only emerges in the consciousness of the Ninth Symphony in the finale, after 45 minutes or so of instrumental music. After a shattering cry and a crisis of dissonance that the whole orchestra screams at the start of the fourth movement, the cellos and double basses reject the music of the previous three. Beethoven samples each of the movements in turn, and the cellos and basses angrily and rhetorically denounce them as not fit for purpose, cutting them off mid-flow. But those instruments themselves aren't up to the task either: the low strings are doing an impression of human speech, but they aren't the real thing. Human voices are needed to deliver Beethoven's real message, and instrumental music as a whole needs to be usurped. The bass solo – the first voice we hear, before the chorus – sings words that Beethoven himself wrote, before Schiller's poem is set. 'Oh friends, not these tones! Rather let's strike up something more pleasing, and more joyful!' – cueing up the 'Ode to Joy' melody, Beethoven's tune of tunes.

The success, and the curse, of the 'Ode to Joy' melody – once heard, never-forgotten, resounding across the world over and over again in concert halls, popular culture, and pageants of national and supra-national identity – is precisely that Beethoven achieved what he most wanted: a song of joy for the whole world to sing. Its popularity comes at the cost of the vast majority of societies on earth ignoring the work it takes to get there: hearing only the melody of the finale, not listening to the existential angst of the first three movements, for orchestra alone, that precede it.

The problem is that if you take the 'Ode to Joy' on its own, it can be filled by whatever ideology you want it to represent. The supposedly apolitical idea of 'joy' has curdled from an embrace for the whole world to an expression of who's excluded, as much as who's included. The melody was used to sound the hopes for freedom and democracy in China in Tiananmen Square in 1989, when students blasted it out of speakers as the tanks rolled in, and it was sung after the fall of the Berlin Wall the same year, with 'Freude' changed to 'Freiheit' ('joy' to 'freedom'), sounding the hopes for the world at the supposed 'end of history'. But the tune has also become an ode to hate, used by the Nazis not to mean that 'all people should be brothers' but that 'non-brothers should be exterminated', as Beethoven's biographer Jan Swafford puts it. It's the anthem of the European Union, but it was also the national anthem of apartheid Rhodesia, while Stalin said 'this is the right music for the masses' after a performance of the symphony. It's not that 'Ode to Joy' hasn't worked as a song that everyone can sing – it's that it's worked too well.

Beethoven's Ninth bears the scars of its history, and ours. And yet its hope and its vision cannot be reduced to politics, and cannot be summed up only in that one tune. The symphony as a whole is a progress from creation myth to a funeral march in its first movement – the old world, extinguished, before the eruption of the most violent music Beethoven ever composed in the *scherzo* of the second movement. There's the balm of the slow third movement, and then the choral pageant of thrilling diversity in the finale, in music that Beethoven borrowed and remade from as many sources as he could, from Renaissance polyphony to Turkish bands.

The community of musicians who come together to perform this symphony, wherever and whenever it's played, realise something more evanescent yet more powerful than political sloganeering, because every performance of the Ninth Symphony is a musical utopia in action. The rest of the world? That's up to us.

PIECE #29

LOUISE BERTIN (1805–1877)

FAUSTO

Paris, 1831

Those dreams of humankind's utopian future emerged at the same time that the European imagination was stalked by a myth that's so intoxicating because it's a mirror to human frailty and temptation, to the split in every human being between pleasure and duty, ambition and responsibility. As the Faust legend and Johann Wolfgang von Goethe's retelling and expansion of it shows, in the end there are just two choices available to us: will we sign the devil's pact, or won't we? Will we give in to worldly fame, fortune, love and lust? Or will we find the other path towards redemption?

It was Goethe's story in *Faust*, Part 1, that took over European culture in the early nineteenth century: Doctor Faust, in cahoots with the devil, winning the heart of Gretchen, abandoning her, fathering her child, and condemning her to death as the hypocrisy of society turns pitilessly against her. Its French translations, which appeared in the early 1820s in Paris, inspired the young composer Louise Bertin to start writing her opera *Fausto*, to her own Italian libretto, a project she began at the age of just 20. *Fausto* would be her third opera, and France's first on Faust.

In it, she would rewrite Goethe to give her drama the biggest punch possible. There is no redemption for Faust in her opera: out of shame and guilt at what Faust has done to her, Margarita (the Italian name for Gretchen's character) has drowned her baby and tried to kill herself; she is sentenced to death and refuses Faust's help to escape the prison where she languishes. Margarita dies, redeemed by the Angels, while Faust is fully in Mefistofele's power, condemned to hell at the end of the opera: 'She is saved,' the angels sing – high voices, performing from above the stage – while the demons and Mefistofele, low male voices from the abyss, tell us: 'He is in my power.' Bertin's music ends with an ironically radiant major-key chord that's spread over the whole orchestra, and the very last sounds of the opera are given to the tam-tam, the sonic equivalent of a puff of smoke.

These sounds were first heard at the Théâtre-Italien in Paris in 1831, even though Bertin had completed her opera well before then. Paris's 1830 revolution, deposing Charles X and putting Louis Philippe, the 'Citizen King', on the throne, had delayed the premiere, and those post-revolutionary politics were essential parts of the fabric of Parisian operatic life, on- and off-stage.

Fausto is an amazingly bold, prescient and unforgettable piece of operatic storytelling. The critics at the time bemoaned its lack of tunes, but they also reported the wildness of its orchestration, and its implacable dramatic power: it was music of 'fierce and energetic verve'. They also commented patronisingly about the sex of its composer: her talent 'has nothing feminine about it ... her sensibility is brimming with energy and masculine vigour'.

Bertin wasn't even allowed to take her bows on stage after the premiere. As a woman, it was impossible for her to be seen as a professional in French society at the time: she was supposed to be a musical amateur, and her full name was withheld in the press – despite the fact that all of Paris knew who 'Mlle B****' really was. She wasn't the only woman to have an opera on stage at the time in Paris – Sophie Gail's comic opera *Les deux jaloux* was still playing, after its premiere in 1813, but Bertin was the more celebrated. That was thanks to her own powers of imagination, as well as her training in classes with her fellow student and fellow musical radical, Hector Berlioz. It was also because her father ran one of the most influential cultural papers in Paris, the *Journal des débats*, with its enormously influential music critic, Henri Castil-Blaze. The *Journal* combatted what criticism there was of *Fausto* with rebuttals that Bertin herself could have written; acknowledging that there are 'probably a few too many brassy effects in this opera, but the bizarre nature of the subject and the need for the composer to preserve the physiognomy of her Mefistofele's charms and his harmonic procession are the cause of that abundance'.

Today it's the radicalism of this score that spears through the centuries. Bertin didn't give the public of the Théâtre-Italien what they were used to. In her writing for the solo voices, there's very little cosseting *coloratura*. Neither Fausto nor the soprano role of Margarita are given vehicles for vocal virtuosity for virtuosity's sake. Bertin writes against convention, making her opera all about quick-fire scene-changes and brilliantly achieved economy. She cuts her scenes like a film director, so in Act III, Margarita's prayers are brutally interrupted by the women who taunt her as a 'disgrace'. Bertin doesn't allow us any time to wallow in Margarita's self-pity; she's interested in staging the horror of the hypocrisy of how she's treated at the hands of the womenfolk of the town.

And it's in her unflinching characterisation of Fausto's hubris and Mefistofele's supernatural cunning that Bertin reveals the heights of her powers. Mefistofele is there even before the curtain goes up on an aged, suicidal Doctor Faust in his laboratory, because the sounds of sepulchral trombones loom out from Bertin's orchestra in the opera's overture. When he finally appears – after Faust has been saved from suicide by the sounds of sacred singing – the devil is announced by piccolos and percussion as well as lowering brass, as if he were conjuring a witches' coven as well as opening up a portal to the underworld.

Bertin sustains this supernatural soundworld over the course of the two hours of her opera, but she knows precisely when to move on to the next scene. She is ruthlessly committed to the momentum of her drama, refusing to allow herself or her characters – or her singers – to indulge themselves. But that's not to say the piece doesn't have stand-out moments of song, melody, psychological reflection – and even of diabolical comedy. Her quartet at the end of Act II is one of the most harmonically adventurous moments in any early nineteenth-century opera, in which all four characters sing across each other in music that cuts from one key centre to another, so that Faust and Margarita's brief moment of happiness is undercut by Mefistofele's cynical seduction of Catarina. Earlier in the act, the devil has some of the fastest patter-singing in operatic history, as he woos Catarina with a grotesquely comic display. Worst of all, it works, and Catarina duly falls under Mefistofele's spell.

In rewriting the end of *Faust* so that he doesn't survive, but is condemned to hell, Bertin leaves her audience with a vision of salvation for Margarita that comes at a terrible cost. Instead of offering hope for humanity, Bertin puts up a courageously unflattering mirror to her age: the curse of its militarism, in the comically martial music she writes for Margarita's soldier-brother, Valentino, the futile hypocrisies of the church, and the patriarchies of her society. Margarita, for Bertin, isn't a passive victim, but the main agent of the drama: not because of how Faust and Mefistofele toy with and abuse her, but because of her fortitude and her faith. Unlike the more famous French opera on Faust by Charles Gounod, from 1859, Bertin's opera is driven by unsentimental radicalism, not saccharine romance. Hers is the *Fausto* the world needed in 1831, in its economy, its unsparing revelation of the fissures in humanity that lie under all those dreams of revolution and new social orders and utopianism.

Bertin wrote another opera in 1837, to the only libretto that Victor Hugo would compose, *La Esmeralda*, based on *The Hunchback of Notre-Dame*, for the grandest stage in Europe, the Opéra de Paris. There, too, her opera was heard as the gigantic achievement it is, but it was also shouted down by claques who said that Berlioz had written the opera's best bits: not true, as Berlioz knew, and said so, as forcefully as he could in public.

Bertin's own Faustian pact was with her talent: born at a time when she was forced to be seen as a *woman* composer and not simply a composer, she worked on instrumental music for the rest of her life, in pieces that are – shockingly – still unpublished. Let *Fausto* take over the stages where it belongs, and let this revelation of human hubris and the diabolical forces of the patriarchy thrill and terrify us in the twenty-first century, just as it did for those performances in Paris in 1831.

PIECE #30

RICHARD WAGNER (1813–1883)

DER RING DES NIBELUNGEN

Bayreuth, 1876

A new world order was not inaugurated in August 1876. In fact, the steam engines used to create the water and atmosphere effects on stage at Richard Wagner's purpose-built theatre, on top of a green hill in Bayreuth in Bavaria for the first complete performances of his *Ring Cycle*, meant that the instruments in the pit were in danger of being rained on by condensation, so that string players, who were especially exposed, were at risk from a literal river of moisture as the Ring was returned to the mythical Rhine at the end of *Götterdämmerung* ('The Twilight of the Gods').

Wagner was distraught and financially destroyed by the real-world compromises of getting his four-opera, 16-hour cycle on stage. He had realised his artistic dream, but the cost of the encounter with the singers, props, audiences and stage-craft was vertiginously gigantic, and sometimes comic. A dragon's head, made in England for the essential scene in the third opera, *Siegfried*, when the hero slays the dragon to retrieve the Ring, didn't turn up because it was sent to Beirut – not to Bayreuth.

Wagner might have been better off if he'd put into practice his initial vision for the ritual of the *Ring Cycle* instead. *The Ring* was a multi-dimensional, nearly three-decade labour of writing the texts and the music, as well as a mighty effort of fundraising and forelock-tugging to King Ludwig II of Bavaria and Wagner

Societies all over the Western world. But, at the beginning, in the wake of the European revolutions in 1848, Wagner had a much more austere conception: the Ring would be staged in a bespoke theatre, and at the conclusion of the performance, the theatre and the score would be burned, so that the Ring would be a one-off ritual sacrifice and world-purification, mirroring the Ragnarök the audience had just witnessed.

The mythology of the Ring belongs to ancient Nordic, classical and Germanic histories that Wagner plundered for his own ends in his texts for the operas, and yet it's a definitively nineteenth-century worldview that comes to life in the trajectory of its drama. Among its essences is the story of how a woman becomes wise: Brünnhilde, the deathless Valkyrie who chooses love – and mortality – to be with the hero, Siegfried (who is also her nephew; just one of the internecine quirks of the Ring's labyrinthine plot across the domains of gods, monsters and human beings), and who finally rejects the power and corruption of the Ring.

That worldview of the Ring is neither narrowly utopian, nor is it merely a dystopian warning about the ills of the modern industrial society that was emerging in the larger nation states, such as the unified Germany that had grown from the turmoil of the revolutionary decades earlier in the century. In Dresden in 1848, Wagner himself had been on the side of the anti-monarchist revolutionaries: he grew up thinking that ideas could change the world and that his music could be part of the struggle for new nations, new ways of being, new kinds of social organisation.

But as Wagner's writings make clear, his worldview devolved into clear ideas of who was sanctioned to participate in this new world, and who wasn't. Wagner's anti-Semitism is a notorious and ever-present fact of his life. He gave his prejudices pseudo-intellectual foundations in his tract 'Das Judentum in der Musik' ('Jewishness in Music'), an essay that was just one of the places in which Wagner set out the characteristics of purity, authenticity and integrity that were the wellsprings of true German art, in his opinion, as opposed to the vanity and shallowness of what he said that Jewish culture and its composers had achieved. He published the essay under a pseudonym in 1850, and reprinted it using his own name in 1869.

The roots of this suppurating, uncloseable wound at the heart of the Wagnerian project go back to Wagner's personal ambitions and his rivalries with two composers whose fame he could not eclipse and whose prodigious virtuosity he never possessed: Felix Mendelssohn and Giacomo Meyerbeer. Wagner harboured profound resentment for their cultural success, which he turned against them and their Jewish heritage, however much he admired their achievements. In fact, during their lives and after their deaths – Mendelssohn in 1847, Meyerbeer in 1864 – Wagner actively stole from them, turning their harmonies and their spectacles into his own.

The Ring's story could have been a black-and-white drama that put on stage Wagner's prejudices and his approach to everything from nation-building to revolution to cultural supremacy. But that isn't where the mythology of the Ring takes us, because it's a multiverse that proves how power corrupts, how lust for dominion poisons love, but how redemption is possible through the sacrifice of the individual and their ego, even if that martyrdom is for a future whose outcome is not certain.

That's the point about the music of the Ring, which is simultaneously one of the most consistent and yet most unpredictable acts of conception and composition in history, over the half a lifetime it took Wagner to write it. Among the spirals of time that its music embodies are the deep connections from its very opening, in the Prelude to the first music-drama, *Das Rheingold*, to its closing scene in *The Twilight of the Gods*, four music-dramas later, and nearly three decades on in Wagner's life. That's a journey that lasts a week in most conventional performances of the *Ring Cycle*, to allow the singers and instrumentalists enough breaks to cope physically with the demands of Wagner's music – and to give the audience a chance to pass the epic test of stamina and surrender that Wagner's music asks of us.

Yet there is nothing truly inexorable about the way that the music and the drama of the Ring work. It's a drama defined by the fateful choices that the characters make: the dwarf Alberich renounces love in order to possess the Rhinegold; Wotan, the leader of the gods, makes a grubby deal with the Giants to win the Ring, briefly, for himself; Brünnhilde chooses mortality and love, but that's a choice that dooms her at the end of *The Twilight of the Gods*.

And it's the openness and ambiguity of Wagner's score that matters the most. For the vast majority of the 16 hours of the Ring's score, he composes music that's in a near-constant state of transformation, in which the music could decide on one harmonic or melodic outcome or another at any point. Wagner's musical language is continuously conditional, allowing for chords to be interpreted in radically different directions. When you're listening, you're suspended in a network of possibility –

like the characters on stage. That's what makes the experience of the Ring so vital: we're engaged at every stage because you feel you never know what's going to happen next in the sounds the music makes, and the choices the characters commit to.

At the end of the Ring – amid the on-stage destruction, the aftermath of Brünnhilde's suicide, the collapse of the realm of the gods, and the return of the Rhinegold to the river – the effect is of a gigantic question: what comes next? Wagner's music doesn't have the answer to the world of humankind that comes after the gods have been consumed by flames. In his score for this scene, the music seems to implode, collapse and coalesce, as if the whole cycle were remixing itself in a maelstrom of memory and entropy. The chain of unanswered questions of Wagner's harmony, and his drama, is posed directly to his audience: what would you do if you had the power to remake the world?

The audience at Bayreuth in 1876 were well placed to answer. It wasn't only Europe's composers who were there in force to experience what no one had heard in full before – from Bruckner to Saint-Saens to Tchaikovsky – it was Europe's and the world's royalty, from Kaiser Wilhelm of Germany to Pedro II of Brazil. The summits of empires were there, crammed in their ludicrous finery into the theatre's democratically narrow and uncomfortable rattan chairs that are still there in the theatre, for the duration of the Ring. And the choices they made about the significance of what they witnessed, how they interpreted its essential lesson that absolute power corrupts absolutely, and that it's not the greed or the gold, but Brünnhilde's love and sacrifice that suggests a real way forward: that was the opportunity they all had in seeing the ritual of *The Ring* at the green hill at Bayreuth.

And it was precisely those ideas that were radically unheard, in terms of the political decisions that world leaders made in subsequent generations. It wasn't the ambiguities of Wagner's drama that Germany's leaders loved, it was the heroism – even though Siegfried is hardly a hero in Wagner's story, betraying the woman he loves, before he's drugged and murdered by the proto-fascist Hagen. Hagen is the closest Wagner comes to a black-and-white depiction of irredeemable villainy in the Ring. And it was Hagen's violence, his absolutism, his denouncing of the past and his lust for power that was the model for what happened next to the legacy of the Ring.

Wagner's anti-Semitism was easily employed as a cultural underpinning for the ideologies of German fascism. Even though Hitler's favourite composer was really Franz Léhar, not Wagner, Bayreuth provided Hitler with the cultural capital he needed to enlist some of Germany's intellectuals to his side – including the leadership of Bayreuth, Wagner's widow, Cosima, his son Siegfried, and his English-born daughter-in-law, Winifred. Wagnerism and its symbiosis with Nazism is a stain on the reputation of the music that, for many, can never be redeemed, and should never be redeemed. That's why his music is still the subject of a ban in Israel, and it's why so many conductors, including Arturo Toscanini in the 1930s, refused to conduct at Bayreuth. That's the echoing association that Francis Ford Coppola uses in his film *Apocalypse Now* when 'The Ride of the Valkyries' – still one of the Ring's most famous excerpts – accompanies the slaughter of the Vietnamese village as the American helicopters, led by Robert Duvall's Lieutenant Colonel Kilgore, blast out Wagner's music as they storm in from the sea: 'I love the smell of napalm in the morning'.

Wagner's own story and the story of the Ring are twin revelations of the dark sides of a truth that can never be repeated enough, and whose resonances only become more powerful as the Ring is performed and re-interpreted in Bayreuth and all over the world: the corruption of power, greed and ego. If politicians had understood and attended to the complexity of the Ring's music and drama – and if they had confronted instead of amplified the racist philosophies of its creator – their political decisions would have been profoundly different.

Wagner's music is a question, for some, and a wound, for others, that can never be answered, and which will never be healed. But its urgency only increases. *The Ring*'s music, and where we choose to put ourselves in relation to its composer, puts us in a place where we can't look away, where we have to take responsibility, for our lives, and for the lives of others. What happens next will be fulfilled in the choices we make, individually and collectively. What world will we build?

PIECE #31

PATTY AND MILDRED J. HILL

'HAPPY BIRTHDAY'

Louisville, Kentucky, 1893

How does a song that takes over the world really begin? Not in a concert hall, like the utopian dreams of Beethoven, or in a bespoke theatre, like the hubristic grandiloquence of Wagner's, but, instead, in a cabin in the woods in the Kenwood Hills, Kentucky, in the USA in the mid-1890s. At a gathering with their friends, the sisters Patty and Mildred J. Hill spontaneously came up with new words for one of their own favourite songs, which they had created for the children of Patty's kindergarten to sing in the mornings. Written with music by Mildred to Patty's words in 1893, it was a song they and their pupils knew as 'Good Morning to All', a simple eight-bar melody in a sunny major key and a simple, swinging three beats in the bar, which the children learnt easily as a welcome to the school day, inculcating the philosophy that underpinned the kindergarten movement at the end of the nineteenth century in the United States: learning through doing, participation, and sensory engagement. In the Esta Cabin that day, however, Mildred and Patty changed the words to celebrate an anniversary, and 'Good Morning' became 'Happy Birthday' – and the world's collective soundscape changed overnight.

That's not quite true: not least because the song, while locally popular, required the technology of print, broadcast and public performance before it could be established not as a ritualised school matins but instead as *the* birthday song of birthday songs, infinitely flexible in being instantly person-alised, and instantly memorable as one of the most effective earworms ever composed.

And that's where things get complicated. Because 'Happy Birthday' became mired in some of the twentieth and twenty-first century's most vexed questions of ownership, copyright, corporate greed and legal shenanigans that were only fully resolved in 2016, thanks to a case brought by the filmmaker Jenn Nelson. It comes as a surprise to any of the billions who have innocently sung 'Happy Birthday' to their families and friends over the decades that, before that date, they should have been paying the publishers, Warner Chappell, a fee for their public performances of the song, and a tune that feels like it's owned by the world's collective anni-versarial consciousness was actually a property to be bought, licensed and sold.

The 'Happy Birthday' song's ubiquity spread from that cabin in Kentucky to birthday celebrations all over the world through the publication of its sheet music, and its use as the first singing telegram in 1933 – you could buy a performance of a personalised 'Happy Birthday' rendition from Western Union's Lucille Lipps. But it was when the tune made it to Broadway in Irving Berlin's review *As Thousands Cheer* that the lawyers really got interested. Mildred had died in 1916, and Patty, by then a leading authority on children's education, said she had 'long ago resigned herself to the fact that her ditty had become common property of the nation'. But Berlin's show was sued for a satirical birthday scene in which John D. Rockefeller's children give him the Rockefeller Center as a birthday gift, while, outside, the Great Depression takes its toll on millions of Americans. The publishers demanded $250 a show, and the suit was settled in 1935: Hill's family claimed copyright over the lyrics of the song.

Spooked, the entertainment industry and retail and recreation outlets had to get creative to avoid the lawyers. Instead of paying licensing fees, everyone from US entertainers to restaurant chains had to compose their own birthday songs to make sure they wouldn't be liable. While out in the real world, 'Happy Birthday' took over family gatherings from Kentucky to Kyoto, on film and TV and in any public commercial space, *ersatz* birthday songs were made by studios and restaurant owners – and none of them stuck. There's a whole repertoire of these sub-'Happy Birthday's out there online, and you can spend many, many unhappy hours listening to them. My advice – don't.

'Happy Birthday' works as a tune because it's a perfectly balanced mix of the comforting and predictable, and the piquant and memorable. And here goes, an attempt to pin the butterfly of the catchiness of its melody to the board of music analysis: its two phrases both finish on the home chord, but the excursions they make to get there in the harmony and the melody are just interesting enough to be stimulating rather than stultifying. The second half of the tune opens up so it spans an octave leap, which is also the whole range of the tune, its lowest and highest note. And in the most commonly-used harmony that sits under the melody at the climactic moment in the micro-drama of any rendition of the song – when the name of the birthday-owner is revealed, whether it's your one-year-old niece, your 100-year-old grandmother, or the 45-year-old President Kennedy, to whom Marilyn Monroe sang at Madison Square Garden in 1962 – there's a little aching suspension, and the dissonance is only resolved in the middle of the bar, as the name is sung over two descending notes, before returning reassuringly to the home note of the scale in the final 'happy birthday to you'.

That's the magic that Patty and Mildred made, a melody conceived not with ideas of money-making but educational generosity at its heart. Those principles were the exact opposite of those that motivated Warner Chappell when they acquired what they thought were the rights in 1988, making them around $2 million a year, and turning 'Happy Birthday' into a cash-cow as well as the sound of the world's celebrations.

So when the filmmaker Jenn Nelson was making a film about the 'Happy Birthday' story, it stuck in her craw that she had to pay thousands of dollars to use the song, and she set out to save 'Happy Birthday' and to restore it to the commons, where Mildred and Patty always wanted it to be. Since the success of her lawsuit in 2016, that's where 'Happy Birthday' rightfully belongs.

'Happy Birthday' is being sung, right now, all over the world, as you're reading these words: it's likely the first communal song that most children on the planet learn, and it might be the only communal singing that families and groups of friends do together all year. And in most performances, the voices across the birthday cake search for a starting note, but never quite land on the same one, so what should be a sonorous unison turns into a deliriously dissonant cacophony, complete with ad lib harmonies and falsettos, if you're feeling adventurous after a toast of something fizzy, from a soda at school to Prosecco at a party.

'Happy Birthday' symbolises more democratically, more generously and more globally our human impulse to sing together than any other tune on earth. It's a ritual that marks time and that seems as if it's always belonged to the world's musical consciousness. Thanks to Jenn Nelson and her lawsuit in 2016, it finally does in law as well as in the reality of our lives.

So, next time you sing it, make a toast to her – and above all to the Hill sisters, whose pioneering educational inspiration gave the world its most sung song, its most celebratory theme tune, owned by anyone who sings it, and by anyone who has a birthday. Which means: every single one of us.

PIECE #32

IGOR STRAVINSKY

LE SACRE DU PRINTEMPS

('THE RITE OF SPRING')

Paris, 1913

All these things are true: there was – and wasn't – a riot in the audience on 29 May 1913 when the ballet *The Rite of Spring* was premiered by Sergei Diaghilev's Ballets Russes company at the brand-new Théâtre des Champs-Elysées in Paris; and it was – and wasn't – Igor Stravinsky's music that scandalised and shocked its audiences the most.

The Rite of Spring, as a performance and a cultural phenomenon, was a headline-grabbing success in 1913 and it's still a visceral thrill in every one of its performances in ballet theatres and concert halls today. That's because its music is an embodiment of the sophistication and the terror of modernism and mechanisation, and it's a revelation of energies that are ancient, primal and animalistically violent. Culture in early twentieth-century Paris was obsessed by the lure of the 'exotic', appropriating and othering the images and ideas of distant times and places in its exhibitions, its art galleries, and its theatres. *The Rite of Spring* was a soundtrack to the times that emerged simultaneously like a bolt from the blue and as an explosion into the musical and theatrical life of the subcutaneous trajectories of an entire continent. In its pulsating, irresistible rhythmic energy, *The Rite of Spring* sounds like an orchestral war-machine, just a year before the madness of the First World War consumed Europe, and Stravinsky's metaphors for musical and dramatic oblivion were turned into horrifying realities.

Stravinsky mythologised the composition of his most influential score. He described experiencing a flow state in which all he had to do was receive the message of *The Rite*'s rhythmic radicalism. Composing the piece in Switzerland in 1911 and '12, he was 'the vessel through which *The Rite of Spring* passed'. That puts the creation of the music in a category of quasi-biological inevitability, but the reality is that Stravinsky's piece does not emerge from nothing in terms of his own life, and it doesn't appear as if unbidden from the musical earth. At every stage and in every dimension of its performance, from its costumes and its choreography by Vaclav Njinsky, to its dramaturgy, *The Rite of Spring* is supremely calculated, and the project was precisely designed to cause exactly the kind of *succès de scandale* that Diaghilev knew would add to its notoriety, and to the worldwide fame of the Ballets Russes company.

By 1913, Parisian audiences had come to expect a virtuosic vision of Russian orientalist escapism from the stories that Diaghilev and his company presented to them, in particular the phanstasmagoria of sound, movement and spectacle that Stravinsky's collaborations had produced in 1910 and 1911 in his ballets *The Firebird* and *Petrushka*. Stravinsky – who wasn't even 30 when he composed these pieces – conjured worlds of fairy-tale magic, culled from mythic and dramatic sources that were familiar to Russians but new to France, stealing especially liberally from the operas of his teacher Nikolai Rimsky-Korsakov in *The Firebird* to find the soundworld of Kashchey, the evil magician, and the Firebird's supernatural plumage.

Petrushka is another step up in theatrical ambition and musical brilliance from *The Firebird*, as Stravinsky turns the characters of a puppet show into the stars of the show, and transforms the human onlookers at the Shrovetide Fair into whirling machines. Petrushka, the puppet, is fully humanised by the very end of the story and by the music Stravinsky composes at the end of the ballet, as Petrushka's ghost haunts the carnival after he has been murdered.

Petrushka is also the score in which Stravinsky dares new directness of harmonic simultaneity, melodic simplicity and rhythmic layering. He makes a music that moves not in paragraphs of theme and development, in the unfolding narratives that European music is so often indebted to, but presents his themes and ideas fully formed from the start, so that his compositional options are either to put them on top of one another, to combine them, or to repeat them in ever-more dazzling combinations of orchestral colours. This kind of juxtaposition, jump-cut editing and sampling of street-songs, hurdy-gurdy tunes and folk melodies, creates a cavalcade that pre-dates and prefigures postmodernism and digital musical culture. (The opening chord of Kashchey's 'Infernal Dance' from *The Firebird* has become a literal cornerstone of digital music: it was sampled by the Fairlight company for their pioneering samplers in the 1980s as a sound called 'orchestra hit', which means that, in hip-hop, techno and house music ever since, Stravinsky – the ur-sampler in how he remade classical music culture – has himself been turned into a sample and been used, cut-up and appropriated billions of times.)

The Rite of Spring maxes out all of these compositional elements. The same techniques from *Petrushka* are there in *The Rite of Spring*, they're just intensified and taken to what seemed to many – including *The Rite*'s first conductor, Pierre Monteux – to illogical extremes of rhythmic stratification and screaming harmonic dissonance. That's true of the subject matter too. For this ballet, Stravinsky strips out the colour and the exoticism from the story to find a savage pagan essence. The dramatic idea is another fictional conjuring of a pre-Christian Russia, but this time it's the dark side of that orientalist fantasy. As Stravinsky said, the two parts of the ballet – 'The Adoration of the Earth' and 'The Sacrifice' dramatise the following scenario: 'One day [in 1910], when I was finishing the last pages of *L'oiseau de feu* in Saint Petersburg, I had a fleeting vision … I saw in my imagination a solemn pagan rite: sage elders, seated in a circle, watching a young girl dance herself to death. They were sacrificing her to propitiate the god of Spring. Such was the theme of the *Sacre du printemps*.'

The calmness of Stravinsky's description belies the horror of this subject matter. There is no love story here, there are no opportunities for *pas de deux* or whirling dances of joyous communion. Instead the earth is pounded and pummelled by the feet of The Chosen One as she dances herself to death in the very final number of the ballet, 'The Sacrificial Dance', after the rituals of the elders and the pagan community have prepared her for this terrible but essential deed, a giving of human life to the Earth so that the violent pageant of spring can be renewed in nature.

One of *The Rite*'s most famous images of sonic savagery is the 'The Dance of the Young Girls' at the start of 'The Augurs of Spring', the first fast music in the ballet, after the chaotic strata of folk tunes and bird song of the introduction. The unpredictable jolts of accents within the repeated quavers, and the apparently uncompromising dissonance the strings and horns play seem to come from a new musical world. But in fact Stravinsky is re-composing the elements of music here, not making them anew. This supremely scrunchy harmony, which has inspired everything from John Williams's music for *Jaws* to minimalist work-outs by Philip Glass, is made by putting two consonant chords on top of one another. On their own, these two chords are incapable of offence, but when you play them at the same time, the effect is bewildering. *The Rite of Spring*'s guiding principle, of a surface complexity achieved through pile-ups of simple individual elements, whether familiar chords or repetitive rhythmic patterns, is the secret to what creates the piece's avant-garde soundworld.

It's also how the piece mirrors the organic world as well as the world of machines. The repeating patterns of rhythm that interlock and grind against one another in the two breathtaking dances at the end of both parts of the ballet are like genetic sequences of musical DNA spliced with one another, creating the terrifying musical homunculi of Stravinsky's score, which caused so many in the audience in Paris at the first night to howl with derision. But the supposed riot that evening – which was probably stage-managed for maximum column inches on both sides of the Atlantic by Diaghilev – was as much in protest at Nijinsky's choreography as it was about Stravinsky's music. The bodies on stage moved not with grace and gravity-defying leaps and bounds as the conventional aesthetics of ballet demanded, but with movements of their bodies directed into the earth, with the energy of clods of dirt, of rock being quarried, of bodies thumping, stamping and pounding, dancing into the earth, not trying to float above it.

The dancers' destination, and the terminus of every performance of *The Rite of Spring*, whether it's in a concert hall or a theatre, is the fatal dance of The Chosen One. The ritual sacrifice that the community of male Elders demands of this young female victim cannot be forgotten, amid all the virtuosity of what any orchestra achieves in any performance of this piece, in the ballet theatre or the concert hall. And in that image, of an Earth and a Spring redeemed by the sacrifice of an innocent youth, whose fate is sealed by the most deliberately non-human music that any composer had composed by 1913, there's a revelation of the violence that the machines of patriarchy have always visited upon the young women of their societies.

The Chosen One also stands on the cusp of the sacrifice of millions in the First World War, and all the fields of Europe and the rest of the world that would be 'propitiated' by their blood and their lives. In its impassivity, and its raising of the mechanistic to the aesthetic, *The Rite of Spring* unconsciously reveals the early twentieth century's savagely inhuman reality. Stravinsky channelled more than he realised: he turned the unseeing cruelty of the machine age into human-made music and dance. *The Rite of Spring* was a ritual for a new musical era in 1913, and it's still a shocking vision of irresistible violence today.

PIECE #33

LILI BOULANGER (1893–1918)

PSALM 130: 'DU FOND DE L'ABÎME'

('FROM THE DEPTHS I CRY TO THEE')

Gargenville, France, 1917

This piece is a cry from the depths of a personal despair and a profound empathy for the conflict ravaging Lili Boulanger's country and continent in the years she composed it, between 1914 and 1917. And it's music that's an answer to Stravinsky's pre-war desecration of the human in the maw of the infernal machines of music and the unappeasable earth in *The Rite of Spring*. In total contrast, Lili Boulanger's piece is a searingly human cry that explodes from the abyss to take over the orchestral and vocal cosmos, a desperate plea for the mercy of Yahweh and Adonai in the text of Psalm 130. It's both fearless – in the emotional rawness and musical adventure that Boulanger finds in the gigantic power and sweep of this 25-minute piece for enormous orchestra, choir and soloists – and fearful, in the places of doubt that she discovers in exploring this text.

It's an honest and haunted revelation of the human experiences that Boulanger's life and work took her through in France and Italy during the years of the First World War. Boulanger died at the age of just 24 from the illnesses she had lived with for many years in March 1918, months before the Armistice, her prayers for peace unanswered. Hers was a short but unbelievably full life, in which she found a musical language that was uniquely able to transmute her personal feelings into music and messages of universally resonant power.

She was born into a family in which music was the stuff of life: her 'dear father', to whose memory her setting of Psalm 130 is dedicated, was the composer and teacher Ernest Boulanger. He was probably not her biological father, and was 76 years old when Lili was born, but he was a beloved paternal figure to Lili and to Nadia, her elder sister. Nadia Boulanger was a composer and conductor who would live until the age of 92, and was the century's most important musical pedagogue at her classes in Paris, training hundreds of composers and musicians from George Gershwin to Quincy Jones, Julia Perry to Grazyna Bacewicz. Nadia knew what she had lost when Lili died in 1918, and she made it her mission to promote the legacy of her sister, establishing Lili Boulanger societies in the United States, arranging performances and ensuring that the legacy of her music would live on.

Yet the power of Psalm 130 has still not been heard enough in concert programmes or on recordings. That's in part because of the enduring inequalities of representation in classical music programming, and because of the patronising view that Lili's was a life cut short in youthful inexperience, so that her promise was unfulfilled by the music she did live to complete. But it's also because of the scale of her setting of Psalm 130, which is composed for an uncompromising gigantism of musical forces: two soloists, the choir, and a very large orchestra, with two harps and an organ. This music's vast expressive and sonic scope is announced right at the start, in a soundworld that belongs to this piece and this piece alone. Boulanger creates a lowering atmosphere from the organ and bass drum, a texture made in the lowest reaches of the orchestra, which hovers on the edge of noise, so that the pitches the instruments are playing are hardly perceptible. These pre-human rumbles begin to gather themselves, and a solo cello and tuba snake and slither their way upwards; a double bass and a sarrusophone (a rarely heard orchestral instrument of uncanny power, sounding somewhere between a bassoon and a bass trombone) try again, striving to ascend out of the gloom, answered by a prayer-like chanting figure.

The friction between these two elements, the primordial sliding upwards and the quasi-religious chants, inspires sounds of crisis, a first climax of terror that slips back into the sonic ooze. The choir appear, with voices of exhausted souls, whose pleas to be heard are despairing: they cannot cry with the confidence of salvation; instead, they sigh in a state of resignation and agony amid warped fanfares and exclamations of hellish darkness in Boulanger's orchestration, the opposite of radiant resolution.

This is a state of desperation that Lili Boulanger knew in her own life. Her illnesses were so debilitating that she couldn't compete for the most prestigious composition prize at the Conservatoire de Paris, the Prix de Rome. But she entered again the next year – and won it, becoming the first woman to do so with her cantata 'Faust et Hélène' in 1913. She was dogged by her ill health throughout the years of the First World War, but instead of casting her down, her illness drove her to participate in the fullness of every aspect of life – romantically, musically, spiritually – and to do what she could for the war effort.

She and Nadia ran a charity, and a newspaper, to help musicians and composers who were fighting on the front lines, and their families, wherever they were in the world. Lili was tireless in committee work and administration, in fundraising and dealing with the politics of the Conservatoire, while also fulfilling the terms of the Prix de Rome's essential gift to any composer, the chance to live and study and work in Italy.

Boulanger had already composed perhaps the most eerily premonitory of all musical responses to the pre-First World War world in 1912, with her piece '*Pour les funérailles d'un soldat*', her 'Funeral ritual for a soldier', for chorus and orchestra, which transmutes the images of public mourning – the muffled marchsteps, the sighing crowds – into a transcendentally tragic pageant, calling and recalling across the ages of musical history, from the Dies Irae chant to the modernism of her time. But it's in her three Psalm settings composed after 1914 that Boulanger turns musical composition into an act of revelation: there's the joyous celebration of Psalm 124, a burst of energy for brass, percussion and voices, that announces the joy of the Maker of Heaven and Earth, and there are the sounds of fervent faith in the face of oppression in her setting of Psalm 129.

But Psalm 130 is on the largest scale of ambition and emotion, and its cry from the abyss is the greatest act of compositional courage in a life that was full of it. Boulanger dares to face her mortality, and to turn her empathy for the hundreds she knew and helped in the First World War, let alone the thousands of victims she read about as the charnel house of the trenches claimed their terrible price, into the substance of '*Du fond de l'abîme*'.

So much of the musical material she writes for the voices is made of the sounds of human cries turned into mandalas of mourning. The semitone, the smallest interval in the Western scale, keens and laments in the melodic lines for the voices, as if Boulanger had analysed the sounds of tears and turned them into music for her chorus to sing. The spiritual progress of Psalm 130 precisely mirrors its musical and dramatic structure, so that the whole piece rises and falls as a series of climaxes of progressive intensification, in music that surges from lyricism to rhythmic overdrive as the heartfelt anguish of the voices longs for redemption and mercy at the hands of their God. Towards the end of the piece, Boulanger achieves a soundscape that seems like that resolution in action, as a glittering halo of figuration surrounds the voices – the cry from the deep, answered at last.

But Boulanger is too morally and artistically courageous to end there: the music winds down to the depths, and the voices intone more of those plangent semitones, continuing to implore Yahweh for mercy. It's a fragile peacefulness that you feel could be disturbed by the beating of a moth's wings. '*Du fond de l'abîme*' dares to look into the abyss: if there is a resolution here, it's provisional, conditional upon how we all interpret the musical events we've lived through – how we all accept and deal with the intertwining histories of our own lives, and the creeping tragedies of the world we live in. With exquisite sensitivity and absolute creative fortitude, Lili Boulanger goes to these places in Psalm 130 so that we might follow her, to have the chance to be transformed – and to transform our own world.

PIECE #34

RALPH VAUGHAN WILLIAMS
(1872–1958)

THE LARK
ASCENDING

Bristol and London, 1920–1921

The Lark Ascending is a piece whose composition and performance frames the First World War, a conflict in which the 41-year-old Vaughan Williams lied about his age so that he could enlist as part of the Royal Army Medical Corps as a stretcher-bearer. The personal experiences, hardships and sorrows of losing so many of his musician friends over the course of the war marked Vaughan Williams personally, just as it left its mark on his music. That's true of his Third Symphony, which he called the 'Pastoral', which is a really a series of laments and transcendences for the generational losses of the war, a pastoral that's a pageant of grieving for the fields of France, and Europe – 'not Lambkins frisking at all as most people take for granted', as Vaughan Williams wrote. A trumpet transmutes the bugle calls of the battlefield in the second movement, and in the last, a wordless soprano sings music that's staged in the beyond, above those fields of France, above their trauma too, in an ether of consolation and meditation.

But Vaughan Williams had already written an elegy for his time in The Lark Ascending, his 'Romance', as he called it, originally for violin and piano, which is how it was first performed in 1920, and in his version for solo violin and chamber orchestra, as it was revealed to the world in London in 1921. Romance: for Vaughan Williams, that's not a word that means sensual love, but a place of contemplation and lyrical profundity – that's what the Romance movement of his later Fifth Symphony does, and that's the same spirit that inspires *The Lark Ascending*.

Yet there is love here: a love for the inspiration of the natural world, the countryside that Vaughan Williams knew not only as an ideal, but which he lived and experienced with his boots on the ground, and with his pint glass raised to the folk singers whose music he would transfigure in so many of his works; journeys that took him to 21 of England's counties, from Essex to Herefordshire to the Surrey Hills he knew the best of all. And there is love here above all for the song that the lark expresses in every 'press of hurried notes' of its calls. Those are words from the poem that inspired this music: 'The Lark Ascending' is an 1881 lyric by George Meredith, which has its own music of rhythm, meter and tumbling imagery, especially in the lines that Vaughan Williams quotes at the start of his score:

> *He rises and begins to round,*
> *He drops the silver chain of sound,*
> *Of many links without a break,*
> *In chirrup, whistle, slur and shake.*

The whole of Meredith's poem is full of musical references, worlds of sounds that are a gift to any composer: the lark's song is 'Sweet-silvery, sheer lyrical / Perennial, quavering up the chord', 'We want the key of his wild note ... truthful in a tuneful throat'. Vaughan Williams could have conjured his Romance by attempting to translate the sounds of Meredith's poem into his instrumental music; he could have approached

Meredith's ecstatic nature-worship as an excuse to make a musical pastoral that was full of lark-song-like mimicry; he could have made music that was, like the poem, a criticism and corrective to an increasingly industrialised world.

But Vaughan Williams does something else: he uses the poem as a chance to create a different kind of musical time. From the start of this 15-minute piece, the solo violin is playing in a place beyond human perception of time, flying free of conventions to make music that's suspended above the earth, that sees the human world from another perspective.

The gift of the poem for Vaughan Williams was not to create a line-by-line musical description, but a licence to float free of the strictures of genre: just as the lark ascends above the earth to experience the world from its unique vantage point, so too does Vaughan Williams escape the orbit of any of the rules of musical form or structure. *The Lark Ascending* isn't a violin sonata or a concerto, it's not a song or a tone-poem – it's *sui generis*, its own shape and its own experience. It's a 'romance' that isn't encumbered by any expectations other than to make its own traces on the musical air, starting and ending with the violin's solos in the sonic stratosphere, filaments of sound we follow up and up into the ether, until we join them in a silence beyond their playing, beyond our perception.

Which would all be musically satisfying but historically insignificant, were it not for the way that this music's signature timelessness is an invitation for our own lives to be folded into its transcendent melodism; and how its unfurling song, set so high in the solo violin's register against the slow-moving ground of the string parts, has become a space in which so much individual and cultural trauma, anxiety, and tragedy has been stilled and consoled. When we listen to *The Lark Ascending*, we're suspended in a space made of musical time that stops the clocks of our real lives, that finds a gap between the brute facts of history. *The Lark Ascending* is the sound of time transcended.

That's literally true in those two solos that frame the piece, as the soloist plays *senza misura*, without barlines, set literally free of the divisions of time that most notated music conforms to. In between those solos, the violinist meets the earth of the orchestra, joins them in rustic dances, and sings with them. In taking their leave of them at the end of the piece in their final solo, the violinist – the lark – is a presence you want to follow, even as the ground disappears beneath them, and they are left truly alone, without any accompaniment from the other musicians at all. The final notes of this out-of-time solo are so high and played so softly on the instrument that you hear the vibrating air underneath and around the notes, the sound of the hair on the string, the air column inside the instrument – the sky underneath the lark's wings made into sound. At the close of the piece, there is no real ending: there is a resolution onto the home note of the piece, but a disappearance on a fragment of song that could go on up there in the vibrating ether, in the place beyond our hearing and our consciousness – the realm of larks, and other spirits. *The Lark Ascending* is an embodiment of how we might want to imagine the veil between existence and non-existence, between life and death.

That's why this music is so popular as a piece to commemorate the edges and veils of our own lives; that's why it's so often used at memorials, and why it's frequently at the top of the charts of the most popular classical pieces ever composed. That popularity is itself miraculous, because *The Lark Ascending* is no musical warhorse but a radical revelation. Composed soon after the First World War, it's a message that finds a deeper truth in all its ongoing resonances and legacies than even Vaughan Williams himself could ever know, as we follow the solo violin into a realm of sonic stratosphere and timelessness. When you return to the earth of your own life after a deep listening to *The Lark Ascending*, you find yourself, and the world, transcended.

PIECE #35

SOLOMON LINDA (1909–1962)

'MBUBE'

Johannesburg, 1939

In South Africa's only recording studio at Gallo Records in Johannesburg in 1939, Solomon Linda and The Evening Birds made three cuts of a new song, '*Mbube*' ('The Lion'). In the second take, the one that was released on a 78 rpm record, Linda's falsetto improvises his part above the deep bass voices, who repeat an unforgettable bass line throughout three minutes of the song, jumping up and down an octave and more with cushiony, comforting regularity. '*Mbube*' is a tribute to the spirit of the lion, who might be sleeping, but will soon rise again: Linda's daughters say that Solomon was writing about himself, that he is the lion waiting for his own time to come – and for the Zulu nation to reclaim their independence.

'*Mbube*' became the most famous song in South Africa, selling more than 100,000 copies in a decade, and spawning a whole genre of songs that imitated its essential features, with a definitive texture of a falsetto voice singing over an ensemble of bass voices. But Linda and his fellow musicians never saw the rewards that they deserved. At the start of apartheid in 1948, Linda, who was born in rural South Africa, and who couldn't read or write, was working packing records for Gallo. This would have been injustice enough, were it not for what happened to '*Mbube*': this is the song that the rest of the world knows as '*Wimoweh*' or 'The Lion Sleeps Tonight', in countless versions that have topped charts in America and Europe from the 1950s onwards, and which the Disney corporation used in its movies and the musical, *The Lion King*. 'Mbube' has taken over the world, and is still the most famous African song ever recorded: Solomon Linda's dream of the lion rising, all-conquering, made musically real.

That might be true at the level of sheer recognition, but the real story of what happened to 'Mbube', of how it became an international sensation and part of the world's musical subconscious, is a revelation not of a twentieth-century utopia of music being shared with the world, but of greed, power imbalances, and the colonial injustices that are part of what has so often happened to the riches of Africa, mineral, material, and musical: they are plundered by other cultures and sold on and appropriated, while the original authors, composers and musicians aren't credited or rewarded.

'Mbube' made it out of Africa thanks to the work of the ethnomusicologist Hugh Tracey, who sent it to Alan Lomax in America, who played it to the musician Pete Seeger, who transcribed it and made a version he called 'Wimoweh', because that's the word he mistakenly heard the bass voices singing, for his group The Weavers. Seeger also introduced the song to TV audiences in the 1950s as what he called a traditional South African melody, teaching it to white studio audiences, sharing it as one of the treasures of African culture that the world needed to know about.

Seeger wasn't wrong about that last bit, but what he didn't know was that the song was not the un-authored product of folk traditions, but the created, composed and performed intellectual property of Linda and his musicians. In fact, the 'authorship' of The Weavers' record was credited to 'Paul

Campbell', a made-up name for The Weavers' creative collec-tive. Linda was written out of his own composition on its first appearance on a Western label.

That was a wrong that Seeger attempted to right when he later found out that '*Wimoweh*' belonged to Linda – he thought he had adequately compensated Linda and his estate after his death in 1962, but the money was never passed on. By that time, '*Wimoweh*' had become 'The Lion Sleeps Tonight' in the 1961 no. 1 single by The Tokens, an all-white male voice band. The Tokens' lead singer, Jay Siegel, sang lyrics by George Weiss, and he claims the melody he sings as his own – but that tune is based on the final improvisational flourish that Solomon Linda came up with in 1939. George Weiss took all the credit for the lyrics – and, after a lawsuit in the early nineties, all of the song's royalties too. His lyric: 'In the jungle, the mighty jungle, the lion sleeps tonight' at least understood that '*Mbube*' had some relationship to an apex predator, but it also turned any of the potentially political resonances of the tune, its desire for Zulu self-determination, and an ever more urgent call for justice in the context of racist South Africa, into an ornament of Africanised otherness, just another chapter in a long history of colonial cultural misadventure.

One of the nadirs of the sound and imagery of 'The Lion Sleeps Tonight' as exoticised fantasy is the British band Tight Fit's version, which stuck to the top of the charts in the UK for six weeks in 1982. You can find a video of their mimed perfor-mance online, if you dare. It's a film in which leopard prints, leotards and the male lead singer's bandana are just the surface layer of a three-minute performance of jaw-dropping cliché, setting the tune to early 1980s synth beats of heart-stopping emptiness; the sound of cash-tills and money flowing to white performers and musicians like George Weiss instead of the actual creators of the song.

This saga of continuous and multi-faceted appropriation, earning tens of millions of dollars for people who had nothing to do with the creation of the original song, proved precisely what Pete Seeger said he *didn't* want to happen, that the treasure trove of African culture should be there for colonists to plunder. The '*Mbube*' phenomenon kept going across the world: the song was a hit in Japan as well the US and the UK – and reached its highest-profile manifestation when the song was used in Disney's film *The Lion King*. As Solomon Linda's three surviving daughters have said: 'We were wounded that the children of the songwriter go hungry ... but the Americans are fat with our father's song. That hurt'.

Which is where the white South African writer Rian Milan comes in: his article for *Rolling Stone* in 2000 was the most visible attempt to tell the world the real story of '*Mbube*', and to find a solution to what seemed like a simple injustice: Solomon Linda and his heirs deserved the money, not 'Paul Campbell', not George Weiss, not The Tokens, not Tight Fit, and not the numberless beneficiaries of its popularity. The legal thickets that this seemingly clear-cut case involved are mind-blowing, and amount to an international process in which some lawyers became very rich, while the Linda family claim they are still to see the money due to them. That's despite Disney agreeing to a settlement after the South African lawyers brought their case against Mickey Mouse and Donald Duck (literally, since the case was against Disney's properties in South Africa, i.e. its trademarked IPs, like

Mickey and Donald), and a trust being established to recompense the family.

Yet the settlement was limited in scope: a one-off payment of an undisclosed amount to permanently close the issue for any future claims over 'The Lion Sleeps Tonight'; if the tune is performed as '*Wimoweh*' and '*Mbube*', the family will receive payment, but the settlement term for the big money version, 'The Lion Sleeps Tonight', expired in 2017. It's estimated they received about 250,000 dollars, a fraction of what the song has earnt its previous copyright holders. And that meant that, when Disney used the song in a much longer sequence on screen in their 2019 live-action remake of *The Lion King*, they didn't have to pay the Solomon Linda Trust anything at all.

When Linda died in 1962, he had the equivalent of about 10 dollars to his name; his daughters have lived in poverty for most of their lives, and their sister, Adelaide, died of AIDS in 2002. 'The Lion Sleeps Tonight' is a song that tells so many essential stories that don't just belong to the twentieth century, to apartheid-era South Africa, or to copyright lawyers. It's a story of how poor black musicians have so often been the victims of the success stories of commercial music, from the origins of whole genres of blues and rock and roll, to individual cases like Linda's and '*Mbube*'s. It's a story of how white colonisers and white saviours have all ended up shoring up the prejudices about the music of a whole continent: that it's a communal tradition rather than an artist-led culture, and that African musicians' stories matter less than the colonisers who 'discover' and disseminate their work.

'*Mbube*' is a tragic and cautionary tale – but the essential conditions that allowed it to happen are still prevalent in the music business. In the practices of commercial music producers and streamers today, the axiom that the people who create the art are the ones who receive the least remains the case, wherever they come from in the world – but especially if they are from poorer regions and marginalised communities. Yesterday's 'Mbube' is today's fodder for the algorithms and the business models of social media mega-companies.

And yet, underneath it all, 'Mbube' lives on. Return to that 1939 original, and hear Solomon Linda's voice soaring in hope and ambition and improvisatory brilliance, and listen to a freedom captured on those microphones in 1939 and released every time you hear it: underneath the Tight Fits and Tokens and Disneyfications, there is still 'Mbube', the lion-like spirit of Solomon Linda – awake, and awoken whenever it's listened to, knowing that this is his song which he gave to the world.

PIECE #36

DMITRI SHOSTAKOVICH (1906–1975)

SYMPHONY NO. 7, 'LENINGRAD'

Kuibyshev, March 1942;
Leningrad, August 1942

Shostakovich's Seventh Symphony was composed and performed in the besieged city of Leningrad, which suffered for nearly two and half years of the Second World War. The piece and its 36-year-old composer became one of the most famous symbols of Russian resistance to the Nazis' siege, after Hitler had torn up the Molotov pact and invaded the country in 1941. Shostakovich was fêted by the Russian regime at the time, and his portrait, complete with his helmet when he was enlisted as a firefighter to help secure the Leningrad Conservatoire, was printed on the cover of *Time Magazine* in the US for its 20 July 1942 edition. The Leningrad Symphony is an expression of creative freedom in the midst of the utter deprivation of the siege that reduced the city and its inhabitants to some of the most desperate hardship that any population has ever suffered.

The performance of the symphony in the city in August 1942 is arguably the single most heroic and defiant act of orchestra-building in the world's history. It was performed by a group of musicians who ignored their starvation and their personal losses to play a performance that was broadcast from the middle of Leningrad over speakers to the Nazi front lines as the guns were strategically silenced by the Soviets. They wanted to show that the city was not dead, that its citizens were thriving enough to play a brand-new, stamina-sapping, 80-minute symphony. For the Russians, the performance of this symphony in Leningrad on 9 August was a thrilling and moving victory of the spirit – and it was also designed as a powerful piece of psychological warfare. The siege would last another 18 months: the symphony did not bring about the end of the calamity, but it did provide a wordless expression of defiance and resistance that every Leningrad resident understood.

Yet those same values, of resistance against tyranny, of hope, of struggle, and of courage in the face of oppression, do not only belong to 1942. This music has been used as an emblem of those same values by successive Russian governments, who want to convince their people that they are on the same side of anti-fascist freedom. That means that Shostakovich's symphony finds itself in a contested position in the twenty-first century: Shostakovich, hero of the siege in 1941, versus Shostakovich, used by Vladimir Putin's regime in the 2020s as propaganda for the prosecution of the war in Ukraine. In a speech in August 2022, six months after the start of the invasion, Putin spoke at the eightieth anniversary performance of the Leningrad Symphony in St Petersburg by the Russian National Youth Symphony Orchestra: 'Shostakovich's Leningrad Symphony continues to evoke the strongest feelings in new generations. It makes them share in the bitterness of loss and the joy of victory, love for the Motherland and readiness to defend it'. Putin was effectively enlisting Shostakovich's symphony, and the young orchestral players who were about to perform the piece, as surrogate cultural soldiers, part of the same war effort that mobilises Russian youth on the front lines. Meanwhile in the rest of the world, the symphony is performed to embody resistance to exactly the kind of autocracy and despotism represented by Putin's Russia.

But that fluidity of meaning, significance and interpretation is built into the substance of Shostakovich's symphony. His response to the war is not a one-dimensional expression of Soviet valour in the face of the horrors of the conflict. His first musical duties in the besieged city were to arrange popular songs and to compose anthems for the Home Guard. That was what the regime wanted, and it's what they got. But the Seventh Symphony was not commissioned by the Soviets, it was Shostakovich's personal response to the war. He started out imagining a one-movement choral setting of texts from the Psalms, but the piece that came to him in the first weeks of the siege turned into his longest symphony: four huge movements that he wrote with jaw-dropping speed and inspiration. The first three were composed in just a few weeks in the summer and autumn of 1941, during the siege; the finale was finished after he had managed to get his family to safety in the town of Kuibyshev, after enduring a flight in which their tiny military plane was shot at by the Germans.

The first movement of the Seventh Symphony lasts around half an hour, and contains one of the most shattering orchestral scenes ever composed. Shostakovich stages the start of the symphony as a purposeful, optimistic march that takes over the whole orchestra; music that makes the sounds of setting off on an epic adventure. It's soon counterpointed by a slower melody, as if the camera pans away from the soldiers to see their families and all their tendernesses, who are also part of this great symphonic caravan moving towards a better future.

And then the music dissolves down to single lines of woodwind sonority, zooming out above the drama to look at the horizon beyond. And it's here that Shostakovich's symphony becomes a place of insidious terror. In the distance, so quietly you can hardly hear it at first, there's the tattoo of a militaristic rhythm on a side-drum. It starts as a tickle on your eardrums, something you can only just perceive above a haze of silence, before a melody begins in the solo flute. It's a tune of startling banality, like a character you suddenly meet who belongs to a completely different symphonic story. And this instantly memorable yet profoundly ordinary tune doesn't do anything 'symphonic' at all. It repeats and it repeats, getting louder and louder as it builds from something you hardly see on the horizon to become a gigantically violent orchestral juggernaut, pulverising the fabric of this symphony from the inside out.

This is a deliberately and satirically stupid tune. It's based on music by Franz Léhar – Hitler's favourite composer – the melody 'we're off to Maxim's' from his operetta *The Merry Widow*. This is the tune that attempts to steamroller the symphony out of existence: Shostakovich's realisation of the invasion of Leningrad. The first movement's moment of true horror is when the heroic opening theme tries to compete with the invasion melody, and is crushed under its tank-tracks. This is the traumatic experience that the rest of the symphony will try to recover from, an image of Leningrad suffering, and of its longed-for recovery. In its three other movements, which are made on similarly huge scales, the symphony laments and dances, and in the finale, the music vindicates the optimism of its very opening moments in one of orchestral music's most jaw-dropping spectacles of hard-won victory.

That's how this piece was heard in its first performance in Kuibyshev, and it's how it was played and interpreted by audiences all over the world when it was broadcast from London, conducted by Henry Wood, and from New York, conducted by Arturo Toscanini, after the score had been micro-filmed and flown in secret out of Russia. Those performances made Shostakovich the most famous composer in the world, and made the Seventh Symphony a readymade soundtrack for the conflict and the hopes for its resolution. Yet even the power of those performances is a fraction of the miracle that the conductor Karl Eliasberg made happen in Leningrad itself in August 1942, when he conducted the handful of surviving members from the Leningrad Radio Orchestra, alongside dozens more musician-soldiers and anyone else he could find in Leningrad's exhausted, depleted population.

As the writer Alexander Kron said about the performance on 9 August of the Philharmonia in Leningrad: 'People who no longer knew how to shed tears of sorrow and misery now cried from sheer joy'. The Leningrad Symphony showed that Russia was unbowed, even in the darkest hours of its Great Patriotic War, as the Second World War is still called there.

But Shostakovich's music was already doing more than being a mere soundtrack of hope, something he could have achieved in a five-minute song instead of an 80-minute symphony. The power of the invasion scene in the first movement is undeniable, but it is not only a depiction of the Nazi war machine. Instead, it enacts a brutalising subjugation of individual liberty under its orchestral jackboots. It's about Nazism, but it's also 'about our [Russian] system, or any form of totalitarian regime', Shostakovich himself said. Talking about this precise passage, he said to a friend that 'music, real music, can never be literally tied to a theme. National Socialism is not the only form of Fascism; this music is about all forms of terror; slavery, the bondage of the spirit'.

That's why the message of the Seventh Symphony remains as resonant in our time as it was in 1942. Shostakovich's courage as an individual, and the infinite courage of the musicians who played it in Leningrad during the siege, is one of the most emphatic revelations of the necessity of human creativity in the midst of our most desperate moments. But it's also why today's regimes can use the power of the Seventh Symphony for their own ends: to claim Shostakovich's music as the sound of the victory they want to win against their enemies. Shostakovich, the Great Patriot, has been mobilised, since Russia's invasion of Ukraine in 2022, as one of the cultural wonders of a country under threat from the 'fascists and Nazis', as Putin calls them, of Ukraine and its Western allies. Such are the curdling blasphemies that the ambiguities of musical meaning can create.

But Shostakovich's music in the Seventh Symphony – and in the rest of his output – resists any attempt to paint it in such either/or terms. The Seventh Symphony doesn't matter because it's a simple message: its meanings are multiple because the whole piece is a journey that reveals that hope is forged in a place of bitter experience as well as individual resilience and collective courage. The Leningrad Symphony belongs to our world of conflict and trauma even more profoundly than it did to the city of 1942.

PIECE #37

MARGARET BONDS (1913–1972)

THE BALLAD OF
THE BROWN KING

New York, 1954;
revised version, New York, 1960

The *Ballad of the Brown King*'s text is by Langston Hughes, Margaret Bonds's friend, collaborator, and one of her inspirations when Bonds faced the institutional racism of Northwestern University as a student. The musician and scholar Ashley Jackson reports that when she enrolled in 1929, the university 'didn't provide housing for its black students, and black female students were prohibited from using the school's swimming pool facilities'. Discovering Langston Hughes's poem 'The Negro Speaks of Rivers' in Northwestern's library, Bonds said it 'helped save me ... Because in that poem [Hughes] tells how great the black man is'.

Bonds's courage in turning up to classes in this racist environment to pursue her dreams of being a composer and a pianist defined her indefatigability. Her life's mission was to make music that would honour her identity as a black woman, and which would play its part in the Civil Rights struggle. That includes a radiantly heartfelt setting of 'The Negro Speaks of Rivers', in which Bonds writes music that burns with purpose, injustice and pride, as the singer joins with the ancestors, as the text says, who have known the Euphrates, the Congo, the Nile, and the Mississippi.

The Ballad of the Brown King is dedicated to Dr Martin Luther King Jr. Originally written in 1954, expanded and revised in 1960, and orchestrated in 1962, Bonds saw it as the culmination of her life as a composer, and her and her mother's lives as church musicians, making music of and about faith. Her ambition in the 1960 performances was to have a record of 'one good performance'. That was a dream that had to wait until 2019 and The Dessoff Choirs's album to be realised. (But the version on the record is an arrangement of Bonds's orchestration for smaller forces by the conductor Malcolm J. Merriweather; Bonds's complete orchestration remains to be recorded.) For a piece, and a composer, whose life was celebrated in her own time, that's another of the all-too-familiar shames of the prejudices of posterity. It has taken until the twenty-first century, decades after her death in 1972, for the beacon of this music to shine brighter.

Days after she died, the Los Angeles Philharmonic played music from Bonds's *Credo*, one of her most vibrant and trenchant pieces, which sets a text by W. E. B. Du Bois, a testimony to her 'Belief in the Pride of Race'. *Credo* contains music of faithful urgency, but in another movement, the piece acknowledges the existence of the 'devils' who oppress black people, and who 'spit in the faces of the fallen'. Those are images of racist violence that Bonds characterises with a bassoon blowing nightmarish orchestral raspberries, with skeletal percussion writing.

There is righteous anger and defiance in that section of *Credo*, and there's a similar pain in more songs that set poems by Langston Hughes, like 'The Minstrel Man' from her *Three Dream Portraits*: 'Because my mouth is wide with laughter, you do not hear my inner cry?'

But that energy is turned to a different purpose in Bonds's music for *The Ballad of the Brown King*. In its nine movements, playing for less than half an hour, Bonds's music is fierce in its gentleness and generosity, and radical in its deceptive simplicity. It's a piece in which her unique fusion of styles, reflecting her deep knowledge and love of spirituals, of blues, and of all of the repertoires of classical music, is brought to bear on music for choir, soloists and orchestra, which is an invitation to all of its listeners to attend to and participate in its message.

The Brown King is Balthazar, one of the three wise men who visit Jesus in the manger. His historical depictions in Western art, and the racist embodiments of him at Christmas time in the rituals of European churches – with pageants including blackface Balthazars to reflect his ethnicity – are among the resonances that Bonds and Hughes want to reclaim in their piece. The alleluias that the choir sing around the tenor solo in the first movement are fervent and hopeful that the message of Balthazar should be taken to heart by its audiences: 'Of the three wise men who came to the King / One was a brown man, so they sing'.

The texts of the early movements tell the Nativity story, set to the subtle inflections of Bonds's choral writing, in which the voices conjure a soft-focused atmosphere that connects us with Mary, Jesus and the manger. Bonds creates a halo in her harmonies, a palpable glow of cosseting connection between our time and the Nativity.

But having set the stage, the later movements put the 'tall and brown' king front and centre, as Hughes asks 'Could he have been an Ethiope? ... An Egyptian king? ... Maybe Arabian?'. It's the not knowing, Balthazar's multiple historical identities, that matters. 'I do not know just who he was ... Of all the kings who came to call / One was dark like me / And I'm so glad that he was there / Our little Christ to see'.

And it's here that Bonds's music, and her creative and political project, is most vividly expressed. That's the legacy that Bonds and Hughes want to create: to acknowledge and celebrate that a king 'dark like me' was there at the first moments of Jesus' life, and that his dignity and contribution stands for the nobility and the rightness of their own cause, of Dr Martin Luther King Jr's, and of any listener today who fights the never-ending battle for equality. Bonds's music for the choir becomes purposeful, even anguished, as the choir sing those lines. In those dissonances and in this movement's final climax, it's as if the struggle is faced head-on – and transcended in Bonds's essential hopefulness.

The generosity of Bonds's mission is revealed in the final movements. After we follow the 'tall and brown king' bringing his gifts to Jesus from 'a palm tree land', the music returns to the memory that 'this was a Christmas long ago'. Yet the song of praise in the very last music of *The Ballad of the Brown King* is situated firmly in the present tense: Bonds's, and ours.

The joyful sounds of alleluia, of praise for Christ the King, are visions of the place of inclusive celebration that was the goal of Margaret Bonds's creative life. In her later collaboration with Hughes, *Simon Bore the Cross*, there is an even more intense revelation of their mission to reclaim the black experience in biblical stories, for the black man who carried Christ's cross. But *The Ballad of the Brown King* is the piece that distils and communicates Bonds's message most joyfully. It's a cantata that choirs should be singing every Christmas all over the world, wherever singers and music-lovers come together in the festive season. The way *The Ballad of the Brown King* bears witness to the global significance and embrace of the Nativity is ever more relevant; just as vital is celebrating Margaret Bonds's life of conviction, courage and creativity.

PIECE #38

KARLHEINZ STOCKHAUSEN (1928–2007)

GRUPPEN

1955–1957;
first performance, Cologne, 1958

As a teenager, Karlheinz Stockhausen was forced to serve in the German army at the end of the war. His mother was murdered by the Nazis as a 'useless eater', because of the psychological condition that hospitalised her, and his father was killed in action in 1945. At the end of the conflict, Stockhausen was bound to ask: what had brought his country to this place? His answer, along with so many German artists, thinkers and writers of his generation, was that the sins of the Nazis were not only the responsibility of a regime, but a whole culture; that the complicity of a supine national population and a tarnished world order had led to the unerasable scars on humanity of the Second World War; that the Holocaust was the product not only of the Third Reich, but the consequence of decades and centuries of prejudice, complacency and intolerance.

The political fall-out would take decades and more to resolve, but for visionary musicians like Stockhausen, there was no time to waste. The urgency of the moment demanded the creation of a new aesthetic world that must have as little as possible to do with the past. No longer was the goal continuity with tradition, but a complete rupture, a symbolic slaying of the fathers of the previous generations who had brought the world to the abyss. As the dreams of the German culture that brought Goethe, Beethoven, Brahms and Wagner to fruition curdled in the ashes of its cities, and as the world discovered what had happened to millions of Jews and thousands of others in the concentration camps, there could be no accommodation with the chauvinist romanticism of the early twentieth century, or even with the sounds of prophetic modernist angst in the music of Arnold Schoenberg and Alban Berg. Those were the sounds of the unforgivable, irredeemable past. For Stockhausen – and in France, for that other young lion of the avant-garde, Pierre Boulez, and for their whole generation of iconoclastic composers – the answer was not to honour the past, but to bury it, and to start again from first principles.

The radicalism of what that meant for a German composer can't be overstated. By the twentieth century, the international culture of 'classical music' was one whose main language was German: 'classical music' was coded as Austro-German, from Bach to Bruckner. But instead of wanting anything to do with that tradition, Stockhausen took inspiration from the most abstract-minded of any earlier twentieth-century composer, Anton Webern, whose music unfolds across time like crystals in the sonic air. And in the French composer Olivier Messiaen's classes in Paris, he found an excuse to go even further in exploring the possibilities of musical systemisation, ways of organising musical material in which it was the structure of sound itself that dictated how pieces of music should unfold, not the tainted subjectivity of a composer's imagination. Where emotion, expression and the subconscious had inspired the feverish dreams of composers of previous eras – a project that Stockhausen thought had failed – he took science, research and technological innovation as the arenas for his imagination to take flight.

But even in these fresh starts, Stockhausen found himself enmeshed in different political and cultural dependencies. His love of the technology of the electronic studio as a place where new sounds could be harnessed to make the music of this supposedly purer world were indebted to the technological leaps of the military during the war. And the CIA's direct financial involvement in the musical avant-garde in Germany – they funded it not because the Americans liked the music, but because they, like Stockhausen and his peers, wanted to help make a world that would not lead Germany back to the sins of the past – meant that he wasn't escaping the systems of power that had corrupted a previous generation, but replacing one set of priorities and power dynamics with another. The difference of totalitarian control to the artistic liberty that Stockhausen was allowed after the war is an absolute contrast, a change from night to day, but it's still the case that his music is indivisibly part of the network of post-war politics as well as aesthetics. As the British musical and political radical Cornelius Cardew put it in the title of a book he published after turning against Stockhausen, his former mentor: *Stockhausen Serves Imperialism.*

Cardew's point is arguable, to say the least, but what can't be denied is Stockhausen's gigantic sense of his own historical self-importance. The cosmology of his ego rivals and even outstrips Wagner's in the nineteenth century. Stockhausen wrote a cycle of seven operas, *Licht*, in which his own family – his children, his two life partners – are enlisted as performers and creators of roles that are both mythical and autobiographical. The entire meta-piece lasts around 24 hours and even includes a piece for four helicopters, in which the members of a string quartet all play individual parts, and it's all based on a so-called 'super-formula', a single melody that generates much of the music. Stockhausen didn't, in fact, erase earlier nineteenth- and twentieth-century ideas of heroic creative subjectivity, he took them to newly cosmic levels in his later life and music.

But that's not where we are with *Gruppen* ('Groups') in 1958. In this piece, Stockhausen writes music for three orchestras, each placed around the audience, and each with their own conductor. These 'groups' play at their own precisely cali-brated speeds and in their own rhythmic languages, and yet they have to be in perfect synchronicity with the other orches-tras, in order that the places where they come together to create huge sonic effects can work. *Gruppen* demands a new virtuosity of ensemble, precision and sound production from its musicians and its conductors – and it deliberately confronts its listeners. The sounds that *Gruppen* makes are thrilling, but they are exciting in ways that owe nearly nothing to any previous repertoires of music. *Gruppen* deals in groups of musical events, just as it deals with groups of players, but the harmonies they make are both more elemental and more modernist than anything most audiences had heard before the first performance in 1958 in Cologne. Stockhausen blew apart the structure of music, atomising it into constituent parts of rhythm and texture and pitch, creating a 23-minute piece that sounds both like an evisceration of the fundamen-tals of music – and their radical remaking. *Gruppen* is a piece in which sounds relate to each other not through the laws of proposition and consequence that defined music before the war, but in the way that stars and galaxies do: they are bound by mysterious gravitational relationships that mean they are deeply interconnected, but explaining exactly how is like finding the truth of dark matter in the universe.

But while *Gruppen* breaks from the past in an aesthetic sense, it reconnects with deeper truths of musical experience. The overall shape of *Gruppen* is inspired by one of the most common ideas in nineteenth-century musical culture: landscape. Stockhausen mapped the peaks and troughs of *Gruppen*'s cycles of time onto the contours of the alpine mountain ranges he could see from his window in the Swiss village of Paspels, where he wrote the piece. In that sense, *Gruppen* is landscape music in the way that Weber, Wagner or Richard Strauss also wrote music inspired by nature, it's just that Stockhausen's piece strips back any conventional trappings of emotional expression to focus on the power of the acoustic sounds of his orchestra.

What you hear in a performance of *Gruppen* is beautiful, baffling and overwhelming. Like being in a centre of a nuclear musical reaction, energy is everywhere, even in the silences between the individual pulses and groups of notes that are thrown at you from all corners of the three orchestras: a volley of percussion, a rasp of brass, a scream of string sound. But it's when Stockhausen mobilises all his forces together that *Gruppen* astonishes. About two-thirds of the way through the piece, the orchestras collide with sweeps of brass sonority that swirl and swoop around you, like a big-band composed by alien life-forms. That's the upbeat to what seems like a total sonic collapse, as if all of the instruments were sucked into a black hole, intensifying and stretching their energy at this musical event horizon.

Gruppen makes violent, scintillating music that is among the most exciting visions of what post-war culture could sound like. From the ruins of Europe, *Gruppen*'s climaxes teem and scream with an energy that will always sound new, because the piece is designed to be a musical universe that produces seemingly infinite energy through a new kind of sonic physics: a place where musical energy equals the mass of its elements, multiplied by the square of its listeners' imaginations. It's music that's in a permanent and essential state of novelty: new for 1958, new for our time and all time. *Gruppen* is what music sounds like after one society has collapsed and another world order must be born.

PIECE #39

LEONARD BERNSTEIN (1918–1990)

WEST SIDE STORY

Washington/Broadway, 1957

Bernstein's music with Jerome Robbin's choreography to Stephen Sondheim's lyrics and Arthur Laurents' book: *West Side Story* is a project made by the artistic elite of a city that's about reclaiming streets and communities that were some of the most contested in New York. In fact, the very squares and tenements in which this story is set, an area called San Juan Hill, were being cleared of the Puerto Rican communities whose stories Bernstein was putting on stage. As they were writing *West Side Story*, those buildings were being demolished, the history of those inhabitants erased, so that New York's glittering temple to the arts, Lincoln Center, could be built there instead. Lincoln Center is the home of the Metropolitan Opera and the concert hall where the New York Philharmonic would play, the orchestra that Bernstein led throughout the 1960s, including its concerts inaugurating Avery Fisher Hall in 1962.

In the 1961 film of *West Side Story*, the opening sequence makes the destruction of San Juan Hill clear: the Jets and the Sharks dance on the rubble of the houses where the stories of countless real-life Tonys and Marias used to play out. Those real people's lives and stories were silenced by forces of cultural modernisation led, ironically, by some of the people who made *West Side Story*, which took Broadway and the rest of the world by storm from 1957.

The reason *West Side Story* was such a shocking success was that in updating Shakespeare's Romeo and Juliet to a love affair between two young people from rival gangs, from either side of a racial divide, its creators were daring a realism and a social commentary that musical theatre hadn't seen in the same way before. That meant the feral energy of Robbins's choreography; it meant Sondheim's language, which incorporated as much slang and street vernacular as it could for the tastes of the time – 'Gee, Officer Krupke – Krup you!' And it meant, above all, the stylistic diversity and openness of Bernstein's score, in which modernist fugues vibe with the syncopations of South American mambos, in which the urgency of jazz mixes with an outpouring of sheer lyricism that makes so many of *West Side Story*'s melodies so unforgettable, from 'Tonight' to 'Somewhere'.

But Bernstein's music is driven by something else, by the sound of dissonance, friction and irresolution. Over the opening shot of the movie, as we soar above Manhattan, removed from the people of the city as those monuments to civic pride and modernity pass beneath us – Columbia University, the UN Building, the Empire State – we hear an ethereal whistle, the sounds that we'll soon find out belong to the gang members of the Jets and the Sharks. And that whistle makes the same interval that Bernstein will use throughout the score as its most important identifying feature, the same two notes that will start 'Maria': a tritone, the most achingly dissonant interval in Western music, the so-called 'devil in music', as medieval theorists called it. For Bernstein, the tritone can be used to disturb, as it is throughout the prologue, accompanied by the menacing finger-clicks of the dancers; when he resolves the dissonance, as the melody of 'Maria' unfolds, it can become a sound of voluptuous sensuality, of dreams of love coming true for Tony.

That musical friction stands for the other unresolved tensions in the whole *West Side Story* project. The first is that none of the creators of the story belonged to the communities they are writing about. This is a story of Puerto Rican immigrants told by America's cultural elite, who would all be celebrated at Lincoln Center even as that project swept away San Juan Hill. That's a friction made even more explicit in Stephen Spielberg's 2021 film than in the 1961 version, revealing the unchosen sacrifice that more than 7,000 people had to make in being moved out to clear the way for Lincoln Center's palaces of culture. There's also an inherent undecidability about the scale and sound of *West Side Story*, whose immediate popularity yet musical sophistication makes it a hybrid musical theatre form, somewhere between what opera and the American musical had become by the late 1950s. That's why Bernstein chose to record his piece with opera stars rather than musical theatre singers in the 1980s: José Carreras's and Kiri Te Kanawa's performances are sumptuously controversial in how they make Tony and Maria into an operatic hero and heroine.

And there's the tension in the piece's story, right to the end: Tony and Maria's love results in his murder. Maria survives, and she is the last in the procession as both the Sharks and the Jets carry his body. On stage, that's an image of apparent reconciliation, as if the gangs could stop fighting, and learn that love might be a greater force than prejudice and racist violence. But the music is telling another story, because under the ethereal sounds of a transfigured version of 'Somewhere', which climbs its way to the high woodwinds and strings, the basses play that disfiguring tritone underneath, destabilising the resolution, reminding us of the tragedy, as if the ground underneath all of the characters were unstable, conditional.

And it's the sound of the unresolved tensions of *West Side Story*, the emotional precipices it puts us on, that draws audiences to this unique piece of music theatre. That ending is also a reminder of the literally unstable ground that *West Side Story* is made upon, the tensions between competing communities and contested visions of our cities, between the supposed progress of modernity and the needs of community, and between a culture's art-makers and their audiences. *West Side Story* is the sound of a specific place and time, made in and made about a few blocks of New York in the 1950s, that's still an essential urban soundtrack for all our cities.

PIECE #40

YOKO ONO (1933–)

'CUT PIECE'

Kyoto, 1964

'Cut Piece': the fabric of this piece and this performance is that its composer, Yoko Ono, asks the performer to sit on stage, and then invites the audience to cut off pieces of their clothes with scissors. 'Cut Piece' is always controversial, since it's in the eyes of the beholders what they want to see: do they perceive women's – and men's – bodies subject to violation and vulnerability at the hands of abusers? Or is 'Cut Piece' a mutually empowering exchange, as Ono first thought of it, in which she gave her audience parts of her best clothes, which she was wearing, and said they should send the fragments as gifts to someone they love? 'Cut Piece' is an expression of violence, or resistance towards it; it's a violation in action, or a transcendence and a taking back control: all of those things, and more.

The score of 'Cut Piece' consists of a set of instructions, like so many of the pieces of the Fluxus movement in New York in the 1960s, which put bodies at the centre of artistic practice, and crossed genres with music and performance art. Yet 'Cut Piece', which can be performed by anyone of any gender, is as much a piece of music as anything else in this book, since it's a recipe for performances that happen in time, in which sequences of actions are to be performed, and in which sound is one of the by-products of the piece: the sound of a large set of scissors ripping through clothing, the ritual of one audience member after another coming on stage to participate in the piece.

Ono first performed 'Cut Piece' in 1964 in Kyoto. Or, rather, it was performed by members of the audience, as they processed on stage to take the scissors and cut her clothes. The symbolism of that act means radically different things across culture and time. In Kyoto and Tokyo, the understanding of Ono's chosen seated position as an expression of deference and politeness was implicitly understood; in London and New York, that same posture confirmed the prejudices of white audiences – and white male audience members in particular – to see Ono as a 'young Oriental lady', as she was described by one critic in London in 1966.

Lost on the majority of American or British audiences is the identification of the clothes Ono is wearing with her soul: the Japanese concept of *kami*, in which objects like clothes are so closely identified with the wearer that they contain parts of the person's spirit. That underscores the ritualistic seriousness of one aspect of 'Cut Piece', in which Ono's sacrifice as a performer is acknowledged, respected and participated in by audiences who understand what her decision to give up her control to them for the duration of the performance actually means. She becomes like The Chosen One in Stravinsky's *Rite of Spring*, but makes every audience member bear witness to their responsibility for their own violence, for their own complicity.

But that is the point of 'Cut Piece', revealing not only how audiences change over time, but the way that individuals react differently to Ono's radical invitation to them to participate in the performance. That has meant racist and misogynist controversy in nearly every performance of the piece that Ono herself has participated in, the most recent in 2003 in Paris, an event designed as a complex expression of a hope for peace in the context of the Western world's invasion of Iraq.

In early performances in Japan, in which she announced to her audiences that she was an 'American avant-garde musician' (Ono was born in Japan but has made her life in America since 1952), she remembers a moment of threat when she thought a man from the audience might stab her with the scissors. In New York, instead of silence and insecurity about the invitation to start cutting her clothing away, there was a disturbing alacrity and even relish that the audiences created in the way they used the heavy-duty tailor's scissors to cut away her clothing. In a video of a 1965 performance, a white American man cuts through Ono's bra strap, seeming to treat her and the performance as an excuse for voyeuristic spectacle.

'Cut Piece' can be interpreted as a powerful protest against the way that women's bodies are abused by the violence of patriarchal power, and how they suffer in times of war. Among the images of the atomic bombs that the Americans dropped on Hiroshima and Nagasaki, you can see the damage to the clothing of those who survived, reduced to scraps and torn fragments on their bodies. For some Japanese audiences, to visit the same kind of destruction on the clothing of a performer is to memorialise that history. As part of Ono's peace activism, that was what she wanted the audience in Paris in 2003 to do as well, to cut pieces of clothing no bigger than a postcard, and to send the fragment to a loved one, so that the chain of memorial could be continued.

There is another version of 'Cut Piece' that Ono has composed, but has never performed, which is still more radical in how it would invite the audience to become the artwork:

'It is announced that members of the audience may cut each other's clothing. The audience may cut as long as they want.' It's a logical – and disturbing – extension of the principle of 'Cut Piece', and it's a metaphor for the dissolution of the boundaries between performers and audiences in all spheres of our lives today, in which we are wounded and in which we wound each other in public, and online, and in which our responsibilities towards each other have never been more fragile, or more costly. Who cuts whom?

PIECE #41

PAULINE OLIVEROS (1932–2016)

'BYE BYE BUTTERFLY', DEEP LISTENING

San Francisco, 1965; Fort Worden, 1989

The American composer, improviser, accordionist, electronics pioneer and visionary Pauline Oliveros made deep listening into Deep Listening™: she founded a philosophy of listening that became a trademark, a practice and a series of albums inspired by a literal epiphany of listening in the depths of the Earth.

In 1989, she and her fellow musicians and musical experimentalists, the trombonist Stuart Dempster and sound artist Panaiotis, explored a disused military cistern in Fort Worden in Washington State. They clambered 14 feet underground, and discovered a space with a reverberation time of 45 seconds.

Which is astounding: 'reverberation time' means the time it takes for any sound you make in a particular space to stop echoing, to stop sounding. In concert halls the reverberation time is around two seconds, giving orchestras a warmth of resonance, but still being clear enough that individual notes and phrases can speak. Forty-five seconds is a relative eternity, a place in which every sound you make rings with its own halo that lasts the best part of a minute. In an acoustic like the one Oliveros and her friends found, you hear the afterlife of each sound. Sounds don't die in the Fort Worden cistern; they linger like ghosts, ethereal presences made tangible. (Mind you, epic as it is, Fort Worden does not have the longest reverberation time of any human-made space on Earth: that honour belongs to the Inchindown oil tanks in Ross-shire in Scotland, with sounds that can stay in the air for up to 112 seconds, nearly two minutes.)

The Fort Worden cistern was the place where the first Deep Listening album was born. Recorded in real time, it's an improvisation in which Oliveros, on accordion and vocals, Dempster, on trombone and didjeridu, and Panaiotis's vocals, are suspended in a halo of their own resonance, creating a feedback loop in which the sounds exist in echoes traced upon echoes. That's totally unlike conventional musical performance. Every new sound can't emerge as a new idea in Fort Worden – it has to take its place and its responsibility amid the echoes of all the previous sounds that that the Deep Listening musicians made. When you hear the Deep Listening album, the effect is uncanny, transcendent, because what you are hearing is the sounds of these musicians taking sonic responsibility for each other: you're witnessing the sound of listening itself.

That listening consciousness radiates throughout all of Oliveros's life and work. In her Sonic Meditations she formulated a series of exercises and meditations that are radical invitations to listen to the world in a new way. Oliveros's approach was more all-encompassing than the experimentalism that produced the American composer John Cage's so-called 'silent piece', 4'33". Oliveros's vision of listening isn't only aesthetic, so that environmental sounds can be appreciated as musically as any of the notes and rhythms that make up conventional musical works in classical traditions. That was Cage's view, and what the true project of 4'33" is all about – it's not a 'silent' piece, but one that teems with the energy of whichever sonic environment it's performed in.

But Oliveros turns listening into something both more gentle and more urgent. The gentleness is implicit in instructions from her meditations, like these from 1999: 'Listen to any sound as if it had never been heard before.' And proving the principle of listening as transformative attention, Oliveros says this: 'As you listen, the particles of sound (phonons) decide to be heard. Listening affects what is sounding. The relationship is symbiotic. As you listen, the environment is enlivened. This is the listening effect.' The urgency is in the political and social implications of the kind of transformation that Oliveros's life was all about: listening to the voices of identities that American and Western culture have marginalised, oppressed and silenced; especially female voices.

Oliveros was one of the founders of the San Francisco Tape Center in the 1960s, where she discovered the technology she needed to realise her worlds of imagination at that time. But she was never thinking of sound only as sound, but attending to its meanings, its sources, its powers and provocations. 'Bye Bye Butterfly', composed in 1965, is a pioneering use of tape delay across multiple recorders. In it, we hear sonic ghosts in the machines, as tape delays are overlayed on top of one another. Those are techniques that Oliveros has never received enough credit for exploring so early, but these are processes that became essential to everything from early minimalism to pop albums, like The Beach Boys' *Pet Sounds* or The Beatles' *Sgt. Pepper's Lonely Hearts Club Band*, which began to use the electronic studio as an instrument in the 1960s.

Yet 'Bye Bye Butterfly' is something else, too. As Oliveros says: '[It] bids farewell not only to the music of the nineteenth century but also to the system of polite morality of that age and its attendant institutionalized oppression of the female sex. The title refers to the operatic disc, *Madame Butterfly* by Giacomo Puccini, which was at hand in the studio at the time and which was spontaneously incorporated into the ongoing compositional mix.' This piece is the sound of the smearing and sinking of the patriarchy that condemns Butterfly in the opera: her betrayal, her forced suicide. The electronic haze is a veil that at first conceals and then reveals Butterfly's voice. You hear the oppression in this music, the violence underneath that 'polite morality' of operatic stories like Puccini's.

But in its electronic soundscape, Oliveros makes the sounds of new possibilities of listening to women's voices: in opera, in music, in society. Oliveros's feminism is as essential now as it was then; and Deep Listening, as an ongoing practice, is as radically transformative a force as it's a gentle invitation to meditate on the sonic world around us. One of her Sonic Meditations says: 'Take a walk at night, and walk so silently that the bottoms of your feet become ears.' What your body hears in that space of exquisite sensitivity turns listening into an art of activism as well as attention.

PIECE #42

EMAHOY TSEGUÉ-MARYAM GUÈBROU (1923–2023)

MUSIC FOR PIANO

Addis Ababa/Jerusalem, 1960s–2023

It's music that floats between genre, it suspends the gravities of conventional rhythmic organisation and melodic construction, and yet this solo piano and vocal repertoire is among the most artfully wrought in the twentieth century. Emahoy Tsegué-Maryam Guèbrou's music has roots in Ethiopian modes, and the country's ancient religious music; it feels related to the modernity of the 'Ethio-Jazz' movement of the 1960s, but it speaks from a place of deep knowledge and love for European classical music, to which the absolute nature of these works, their crystalline conception and their performances on her recordings, is most indebted.

Listen to the opening of the first track that Emahoy recorded, in Cologne in 1962: 'The Homeless Wanderer' spins a melody in the right hand that takes on the improvisatory spirit of Chopin into worlds of musical feeling that no one had charted before. Emahoy often uses scales that sound to ears used to Western music like they make reference to major and minor keys, but her music is full of refractions of those more resonant Ethiopian modes, which split the octave in ways that fly free of narrow major-minor magnetism. That's among the musical wonders that give this piece, and everything she wrote and recorded, a spirit that belongs to her music and to no one else's.

The title 'The Homeless Wanderer' stands for some of the stories of Emahoy's remarkable life. Born in Ethiopia in 1924 to one of the country's most important diplomatic families, she was sent to Switzerland for her schooling, during which time she found the classical music she loved – Beethoven, Mozart, Chopin – before she returned to Ethiopia to work for Haile Selassie's regime. When the Italian fascists staged their coup, she and her family were forced to live in exile in Italy. She returned with the restitution of Selassie's government, but her attempt to study in London in 1946 at the Royal Academy of Music was unaccountably thwarted.

In Kate Molleson's moving account of their meeting in 2016 in her book *Sound Within Sound*, Molleson says that Emahoy would never reveal the reason she wasn't given permission to travel. It seems an extraordinary injustice that one of the most talented and well-connected members of Ethiopian society should have this request turned down. The effect on Emahoy's life was catastrophic: she didn't eat, she was hospitalised, and seemed close to the end of her life. But, at that moment, she experienced a powerful spiritual epiphany, and she decided to become a nun and live in almost complete isolation in a monastery on the top of Ethiopia's most sacred mountain, where part of Christ's cross is said to be interred.

She walked barefoot for ten years, and she lost her connection to music in order to give herself to religious devotion. Returning to Addis Ababa in 1956, she found that her father had died and her mother had also become a nun. But the next few years of relative calm in her life, in which she found the piano again, proved to be only the start of the next stage of the upheaval of her life. After the Marxist-Leninists took over Ethiopia, she began to visit Jerusalem, where, in the Debre Genet monastery, she lived from 1984 until her death in 2023.

Emahoy's life charts a story of extraordinary cultural and political turmoil. And it's how her music is simultaneously a still centre at the heart of her world and a uniquely multi-faceted expression of everything that she experienced that matters. She has a way of playing and writing for the piano that touches on so many regions of musical and geographical culture, and is yet completely itself. 'The Homeless Wanderer' is a moving expression of that inbetween-ness, yet there is nothing undecidable or unlocatable about its power and immediacy. The apparent simplicity of her musical materials – the way that bass lines gently undulate, up and down, the skirling melodies in the right hand – is an illusion, because nothing in this music moves predictably or conventionally. Listening to Emahoy's music is like being caught in an ecstatic moment, which unfurls over the duration of each piece. You're swept up in the experience of the music, charmed by its surface and then dazzled and breathtaken by how it moves so idiomatically, so unlike any other composed repertoire of solo piano music of the twentieth or any other century.

When she recorded her first album in Germany, she was staying in Bonn near Beethoven's house. Her piece 'Homage to Beethoven' sounds, on the surface, nothing like Beethoven's music – apart from a harmonic turn towards the end that's like a reclaiming of Beethoven's cadential moves on her own terms. But this piece finds something deeper and truer than any act of recomposition or reflection on the pieces of Beethoven's she played and loved. Instead, her composition finds an absolute originality and integrity, in the way the melody journeys on fractal peregrinations, and the way the bass line talks a walk across the conventions of musical time, insisting on a swinging rhythmic freedom instead of a straitjacket of metrical squareness.

The titles of Emahoy's pieces – such as 'Homesickness', 'Song of the Sea', 'Golgotha' – are clues to the real-life experiences they're based on: her devotion, her stormy travelling across the sea, her intense sense of displacement. But the sounds they make are a pacification of those feelings, not an indulgence in them. Emahoy's music is suffused by generosity, towards herself, her country, and humanity as a whole.

As she told Kate Molleson, she wanted her music to be shared as widely as possible, for her records to be published, and her music to be printed. Thanks to the Israeli musicians Maya Dunietz and Ilan Volkov, that's now started to happen. And while, as Molleson says, 'no notation could really begin to capture her intangible lilt', the gossamer physicality of how she bends time and touch in her playing, her music is now a repertoire not only of recordings, but of potential performances. The invitation to play Emahoy's music, and to be played by it as a listener, is irresistible. Take it, and journey with her to places that music has never been before, across continents, across genres and styles, surfing aeons of time to find a scintillating present tense.

PIECE #43

SONGS OF THE HUMPBACK WHALE

Recorded by Roger Payne, 1970;
cetacean creators from c. one million
years ago–present day

It has only been since 1970 that most of the world has heard them: the sounds, the songs, and the communication of the humpback whale. At that time, there were around 5,000 humpback whales left in the oceans, after centuries of industrialised whaling had butchered them in vast numbers. In the 1970s alone, 363,661 whales of all species across the world were killed. It took a US Navy engineer, Frank Wadlington, who recorded sounds from a hydrophone 35 miles off the coast of Bermuda, to wonder about the weird sonic richness he heard at the same time as the migration of a small humpback population: were the whales making these sounds? The curiosity of the biological scientist Roger Payne brought him and his wife, Katy, to Frank's listening station. As Tom Mustill reports in his book, *How to Speak Whale*, they listened together in the noisy hull of a boat, tears streaming down their cheeks as they realised they were hearing whalesong, and identifying it as such for the first time in human history: 'We were just completely transfixed and amazed,' Katy said.

Roger Payne released Wadlington's recordings as *Songs of the Humpback Whale* in 1970. And no collection of recordings has ever had such a direct impact on humanity's relationship with the natural world. It wasn't seeing the whales, it wasn't knowledge of the 3 million whales that the twentieth century's whalers killed, and it wasn't even encountering their corpses when a massive humpback or sperm whale washed ashore on beaches all over the world: none of that was enough to wake us up to their plight. It took the empathy of listening to them, hearing the complexity and richness and wonder of their songs, thanks to Roger Payne's advocacy, for conservation movements like Save the Whale to be started, and for the International Whaling Commission to turn from an organisation that used to set an appropriate number of whales to be killed every year to calling for a ban on all whaling in 1982.

A connection was made between us and the whales via this bridge of sound. The composer R. Murray Schafer's definition of the perception of sound as 'touching at a distance' has rarely been so accurate: human souls swelled in astonishment at the sounds the whales made, their whistles, moans, groans, clicks and melodic contours spanning the gamut of our frequency-perception as human beings. The world vibrated in sympathy with these humpback whales, and from where their numbers were perilously close to extinction in 1970, they have recovered to an international population of around 135,000 today.

And that population sings. In the humpbacks, it's mostly the males of the species who perform – at least as far as science has yet discovered. And they are singing shared repertoires of song in performances that stretch across their migration routes, the longest of any mammal on Earth. These repertoires of whale-composed pieces are tangible, and ever-changing. Researchers now know that males of the population meet at nodal points along their migration routes, and they sing together. They listen to one another, and accommodate new features in their song that are taken up by larger groups, and passed on to other communities. Humpback whales do not have anything like a single identifiable song, a call that remains constant across the species and across time, as most birds do – cuckoos are always identifiable as cuckoos because of their spring-song, unchanged over millennia. Whales sing a repertoire that's shared across their communities, but which is always developing whenever they meet.

The physics of how they sing are astonishing: the whales hang vertically down in the water column to perform, coming up only to breathe and to return to their song exactly where they left off. As Roger Payne discovered, they time their breaths just like human beings to cause minimal disruption to the sense and flow of the song, and they repeat that season's song for hours or even days. It was Payne's recognition that the whales use internal groupings of sounds in a precise order, and that they repeat whole sections, that led him to designate these sounds as 'song', since everything they're doing conforms to that definition in our human music.

Yet in so many other ways, whalesong remains essentially and miraculously enigmatic. Tom Mustill's book is, in part, a journey towards a still-unreachable goal of meaningful inter-species communication: if we could speak or sing whale, what would we learn? And what would we choose to sing to them? But the mystery is also part of the meaning. Whales' bodies are designed to produce, to resonate with, and to feel sound in ways that make our human bodies seem positively antediluvian. Sperm whales produce the loudest sounds of any animal on Earth, making clicks that reverberate at 230 decibels, and evolution has designed their gigantic bodies, and their massive heads in particular, to work as resonating chambers to allow these clicks to be as deafening as they are, and to travel for hundreds of miles underwater, since sound travels four times as fast under water as it does in air.

In the vastness of the ocean, whales' dominant sense is sound, not their relatively poor vision or sense of smell. And they feel sound as a 360-degree sensation, all around their bodies, an ever-changing sonic sensorium that connects them viscerally with every resonance in the sea. They swim through a whole-body picture of sound. For the entire cetacean branch of life, from toothed whales including dolphins and porpoises to baleen filter-feeders, their worlds of sound are more sophisticated, more subtle, and more strange than anything we can ever experience as humans.

For the humpbacks, the descendants of the singers recorded by Frank Wadlington and sent into the world by Roger Payne, the biggest questions of 1970 remain unanswered: are they communicating to find or impress their mates – their friends, and the females of the species? Are they sharing information about migration routes? Or – most controversially, and most wonderfully – are they doing what we do as humans, and singing for pleasure, for the joy it brings their bodies, for the singing communities they create, for the thrill of being part of a choir of singers that girds the globe in the world's largest choral performance, which has been going on for the million years that humpbacks have existed?

Those questions open endless journeys of research, and they also sound a clarion call of inter-species listening that the world of environmental politics is still coming to terms with – let alone the musical inspiration these sounds have provided everyone from Bob Dylan to generations of new-age and experimental musicians.

A record, an environmental movement, and a story of meaningful and hopeful change: those Bermudan whales, singing more than half a century ago, are responsible for all of that and more. The whales must keep singing, and we must keep listening.

PIECE #44

JULIUS EASTMAN (1940–1990)

'STAY ON IT'

New York, 1973

The American composer Julius Eastman said that he wanted to live his life 'black to the fullest, a musician to the fullest, a homosexual to the fullest'. His music and his life reflects a radical vision for musical culture, especially (so-called) classical and (so-called) avant-garde scenes. Eastman's is a music of human relationships, of ebbs and flows and gives and takes, and it's a commitment to the ecstatic moment of performance. 'Stay On It' is a transfiguration of disco in what it asks from its performers and in its commitment to its groove, its repeated riffs and incessant rhythms, and it's also a more inclusive kind of minimalism than the machines and processes of composers like Steve Reich and Philip Glass in New York were up to in the 1970s.

Eastman lived his life at the centre of so many musical stages: the avant-garde, performance art, the classical mainstream and the experimental leading edges, as well as his career as a recording artist, working with everyone from Meredith Monk to Peter Maxwell Davies to the disco firebrand Arthur Russell. Yet he was in danger of being forgotten at his death in 1990. It took months for the news to reach even his friends in the downtown scene in New York, so the first obituary didn't appear until 1991. In *The Village Voice*, the music writer Kyle Gann lamented the fact that Eastman's scores of so many of his pieces were lost: a symphony, piano music, ensemble works, so much of a lifetime's activity.

That was true even of the pieces that made his name and notoriety in the 1970s, like the pieces he performed for multiple pianos: 'Gay Guerrilla', 'Evil N***er' and 'Crazy N***er'. Those titles were deliberately provocative – and not starred out in the originals. Eastman's aim, as you can hear him explaining in a spoken introduction to a performance at Northwestern University in his beautiful, resonant voice, was to reclaim those words on his own terms. For him, the n-word related to a fundamental quality, a 'basicness' of the field slaves on whose backs American economic superiority had been built. Eastman hoped to become a guerrilla for 'gaydom', as he says, as someone who sacrifices 'his life for a point of view'.

You hear the anger, the intensity and the desperation of that work of reclaiming, historical and personal, in every moment of these pieces, as Eastman asks his musicians to batter at the limits of what pianos can do, with fearsome volume, energy and repetitive power. In 'Gay Guerrilla', the piece builds towards Martin Luther's teutonic protestant hymn, 'A Mighty Fortress is Our God', its meaning as one the straightest tunes in classical music subverted and its power turned towards becoming an anthem of Eastman's political 'gaydom'. But you also hear the desolation, the echoes that can't be stilled, in the splintery aftershocks at the end of 'Evil N***er', and in the halo of dissonance at the end of the nearly hour-long 'Crazy N***er'.

After he didn't get a job at Cornell University in 1983, Eastman became dependent on drugs. He was homeless, and he died alone in hospital at the age of just 49. It's taken decades of rediscovery to reveal Eastman's music, and to find his scores – like the manuscript of his largest-scale orchestral work, his Second Symphony, a searing lament subtitled 'The Faithful

Friend: The Lover Friend's Love for the Beloved' – and for musical culture across the world to catch up with the urgency of his achievement.

Eastman composed using his own technique of what he called 'organic music', in which every element of the previous parts of a piece would be present in each new section, but reconfigured, remixed, and recomposed according to his rational but intuitive compositional ideas. It's that process that's at work in 'Stay On It'. Eastman creates an environment in which his performers are free as individuals, yet dependent on each other. Eastman composes the main material and shape of the piece, and outlines how the musicians should respond when they hear particular notes, shapes and repetitions. He doesn't write a score in which every second is pre-determined. Instead he chooses to put the musicians' listening relationships first, and the precise sequence of notes in any performance of 'Stay On It' second. Before a performance of the piece in Glasgow in 1974, Eastman told the audience that 'Stay On It' was written to use the musicians' most important innate ability: their 'hearing', their listening to one another, and their sensitivity to respond to his instructions and to each other in the real time of performance.

As well as creating this radically relational way of working and performing, 'Stay On It' restores 'the beat', as he puts it in Glasgow, to classical music. The groove you hear in 'Stay On It' is announced right at the start, with a riff that sounds straight out of disco, even if it's played on acoustic instruments. But as the piece moves through time, 'Stay On It' moves the groove from the foreground to the background. It's repeated so often it becomes an earworm you can't escape when you're listening, so that even when Eastman reduces it to fragments, stripping it back to ghosts of percussion and piano chords by the end of the piece, it's still playing in your mind.

These processes of music-making – communal, interactive, generative and organic in their performance and their listening as well as their composition – are the musical expressions of Eastman's individual identity. Or rather, his identities, as a black, gay, avant-garde musician. In 'Stay On It', in 'Gay Guerrilla', and even in his Second Symphony, Eastman turns his ensembles into musical communities that realise the same iconoclastic energy that he wanted his life to express.

Eastman turned the institutions of the classical and the avant-garde to his own ends to realise his own delirious dreams. That's why his music, and his life, are both of their time and prophetic of today's debates around identity, the arts and politics. 'Stay On It' is a piece that requires you to stay with its message of unbounded musical, artistic and cultural freedom, and to stay with the rest of Julius Eastman's music too.

PIECE #45

STEVE REICH (1936–)

DIFFERENT TRAINS

New York, 1988

'If anybody came to me and said, "We'd like you to write a piece about the Holocaust," I would run, not walk, in the other direction as fast as is humanly possible. I think it's an absolutely horrendous idea to write a piece about the Holocaust, and I would be totally unequipped to do it.' That's Steve Reich talking in 2001 about *Different Trains*: his piece for amplified string quartet, sampled spoken voices, and a pre-recorded ensemble of multiple string quartets that the live musicians play with and against in performance, written for and premiered by the genre-busting Kronos Quartet in London in 1988.

And yet this is a piece that's been called, by the musicologist Richard Taruskin, 'the only adequate musical response – one of the few adequate artistic responses in any medium – to the Holocaust'. How can *Different Trains* both be a piece whose composer can say it's not about the Holocaust, and yet can be heard by listeners like Taruskin, and millions of others, as a life-changing testimony of the power of art to connect and confront us with the genocide of the Holocaust, and its ongoing traumatic resonance?

It's because of the fusion of voices in *Different Trains* – real-life, documentary voices, including three Holocaust survivors – that are the inspiration and musical catalyst for everything contained in the three movements, which play without a break for nearly half an hour. And it's because in making art that dares to represent the testimony of those who lived through it, Steve Reich meditates upon rather than dramatising their experiences, respecting the facts of the Holocaust while making something new.

Different Trains doesn't start with anything so direct as a reference to the Holocaust. It begins with strings chugging in rhythmic unison, setting out tracks of semiquavers; over which a train bell chimes and a steam whistle hoots. There's a sudden, jolting change of tempo, and then we hear a voice, not singing, but speaking: 'from Chicago – from Chicago to New York'. The contours of the voice – the melody of its speech, the rise and fall of the intonation of the words – are followed and traced by the strings. So much so, that when you've heard it a few times, the voice seems to be singing; and in a parallel illusion, the instruments seem to be speaking.

This is the voice of Reich's childhood governess, Virginia Mitchell, one of the five speaking voices you hear throughout *Different Trains*. When he was a tiny child, Virginia took him on those trains from Chicago to New York, and all the way to Los Angeles. In 1938, Reich's parents separated when he was just one year old, so he and Virginia crossed the country every year, from New York, where his mother lived, to California to see his father. Throughout the years of the Second World War, he spent six months of each year on either side of the States. As Reich says: 'I thought, '37, '38, '39 … what's going on then? Well, what's going on at that time was that other little [Jewish] boys like me who were born in Düsseldorf or were born in Rotterdam or were born in Budapest were taking trains to Poland' – to the concentration camps. 'And then I – almost against my will – I thought, "That's the piece."'

Reich then went to the archive of voices of Holocaust survivors at Yale University. Listening for days, he found the testimony of Rachella, Paul and Rachel, whose speech melodies spoke most powerfully to him. Once he'd had the epiphany of connecting his trains with those different trains in Europe, the composition process took him over, putting him in precisely the place he said he didn't want to be: writing a piece about the Holocaust.

By the late 1980s, Reich was one of dozens of creative artists, including composers, who had made the Holocaust and its memorial their compositional subject. The German-Jewish composer Arnold Schoenberg was one of the first: exiled since 1933 in the US, Schoenberg composed his *A Survivor from Warsaw* in 1947, which contains some of the most unbearably intense sounds of the twentieth century. *A Survivor from Warsaw* is based on an uprising in the Warsaw Ghetto, and it ends with the words of the Jewish prayer, the Shema Yisrael, sung by a male-voice chorus. Before then, there is only unflinching horror – the sounds of oppression, the voices of the German guards, counting out the numbers to be taken to the camps. The Shema Yisrael is a sound of transcended terror at the end of this devastating cantata.

For Richard Taruskin, Schoenberg's melodrama falls into the pitfalls of Holocaust art-making: 'Were its musical idiom not safeguarded by its inscrutability, its B-movie clichés – the Erich von Stroheim Nazi barking "Achtung," the kitsch-triumphalism of the climactic Jewish credo – would be painfully obvious.'

In Russia in 1962, Dmitri Shostakovich composed his Thirteenth Symphony, known as 'Babi Yar'. It's based on poetry by Yevgeny Yevtushenko, on the Nazi massacre of more than 30,000 Jews in two days in 1941 in Babi Yar, a naturally occurring ravine outside Kyiv. At the time, the Soviets wanted to forget the massacre ever happened. Shostakovich's music and Yevtushenko's words are a reproach to remember: 'I am each old man who was shot here – I am each child who was shot here', the text says, to Shostakovich's music that's an unflinching mirror of inhumanity to those who would rather forget than confront the past.

The paradox is that Reich's music in his Holocaust piece doesn't make sounds of obvious horror or even more obvious drama, like Schoenberg and Shostakovich do. *Different Trains* is reflective and questioning, yet the voices in the music are directly telling us the horrifying facts of the Holocaust. How can Reich possibly use these phrases of Rachella's testimony – 'Lots of cattle wagons there – they were loaded with people – they shaved us – they tattooed a number on our arm – flames going up to the sky – it was smoking' – without trivialising their meaning, without making a musical travesty of the words of a Holocaust survivor?

This is how: Reich makes the sampled train sounds screech around the string quartet's music, while Rachella's voice is cut up into phrases, repeated in the speech melodies in the instruments. Reich uses all of this compositional artifice – sampling, cutting-up, repeating, fragmenting – and yet he doesn't dramatise Rachella's words. He doesn't try to make smoke or flame through musical depiction; he doesn't attempt to make us hear the tattoo needle, the screams of pain, or see the queues of victims having their hair shorn.

Instead, Reich manipulates Rachella's sentences, in how they're cut up and repeated, only to honour them as compositional material and as words that must make us think. They are phrases that pass in seconds in speech, yet they last minutes in *Different Trains*. Reich's setting of them is an invitation for us all to hear them, and reflect on what they really mean: listening to the real voice of a survivor, made more powerful and more direct precisely through the artificiality of Reich's composition.

The very last sounds in *Different Trains* are inspired by the speech-melodies of more words of Rachella: 'there was one girl who had a beautiful voice – and they loved to listen to the singing, the Germans / and when she stopped singing they said, more, more, and they applauded'. Reich doesn't set these words as Shostakovich or Schoenberg would have done – with drama and musical rhetoric and cinematic flourish. Instead, he sets them free as melody and meaning in themselves. The marriage between the instruments and the recorded voice means that the instruments don't obscure her words: they trace the contours of her voice in sonic sympathy.

At the end of a performance of *Different Trains*, the question is: how do we feel, how are we supposed to feel? The electronic echoes of the string quartet in the final seconds of *Different Trains* stand for the echoes of those millions of voices we can't hear and will never hear, including the girl whom the Germans wanted to sing, 'more, more'. *Different Trains* says to all of us that we must not forget – not then, in 1988, and not now. Reich finds the most eloquent solution to the responsibilities of Holocaust history and making a piece of art that honours it. At a time in which history isn't only repeating but running in ever-decreasing circles of time and intensity, our best hope is in our reflection, our understanding, our listening, and our bearing witness to those voices, and to those *Different Trains*.

PIECE #46

MEREDITH MONK (1942–)

ATLAS

Houston, 1991

An opera based on the life of one of the nineteenth and twentieth century's great explorers, composed by one of the twentieth and twenty-first century's most radically explorative composers and performers: Meredith Monk's *Atlas* is an opera that challenges and renews the art form, conceived by a musician whose creative focus and collaborative generosity offers a new way forward for classical music culture.

But *Atlas* does much more than that. Because the sounds that Meredith Monk and her ensemble make in this piece are a plumb line to deep truths about all of our human bodies and voices, connecting us with our oldest cultural genes as a species. And yet these are also sounds which are dazzlingly and fiercely contemporary. *Atlas* was first performed in Houston in 1991, but its resonances, and its embodied musical and dramatic truths contain answers to some of our sharpest questions today. In a time of digital fracture and of fictions masquerading as fact, *Atlas* offers a pageant of emotional and corporeal truths that only our bodies can create and interpret. *Atlas* is a journey of musical discovery, and it's a map of what it means to express our humanity through our voices.

That is the core truth of Meredith Monk's creative life, ever since her epiphany in her twenties that her voice contained all she needed for a lifetime's creative exploration. She says that her voice is her 'soul's messenger ... pick and shovel ...

playground ... radar ... compass ... link to the unknown ... link to the always known ... link to forever ... link to now'. The impact was profound because she realised 'that within the voice are myriad characters, landscapes, colors, textures, ways of producing sound, wordless messages. I intuitively sensed the rich and ancient power of the first human instrument and by exploring its limitless possibilities I felt that I was coming home to my family and my blood'.

And although she uses her own voice, her own 'first instrument' as the basis of an artistic practice that's utterly her own, the principle of her work is that her own voice stands for the possibilities of all of our voices, too. The same voice that Enheduanna raised in honour of the spirit and sensuality of her faith in Sumeria, the same voices that the First Peoples of Australia use in their Songlines, the same voice that Hildegard of Bingen used to chart her visions, and the same voices that Monteverdi and Strozzi called upon in their operas and songs, the same voices that have wailed and cried and sounded out the ecstasies and extremes of our joys and laments: Meredith Monk's voice and her unique methods of composition and performance use them all.

In *Atlas*, there's a dramatic journey that takes in comedy and horror, as the heroine, Alexandra, chooses her companions and meets Hungry Ghosts and Ice Demons, and it means a scale of vocal production that includes everything from spoken voices to whistles and ululations, from cacophonies of vocal polyphony to hauntingly ethereal high register lullabies. The story is loosely inspired by the extraordinary life of Alexandra David-Néel, who travelled the world from France, learning Sanskrit and Tibetan, living in India, journeying to

271

the forbidden city of Lhasa, and converting to Buddhism. She spent her last years in France, learning and working throughout her 101-year-long life.

Meredith Monk abstracts Alexandra's story into a journey that's driven by the character's curiosity to discover the unknown, but whose final image is of a person who has achieved the wisdom to find the wonder in the things of everyday life, sitting at a table, drinking a cup of coffee. The conventional categories of musical culture and tradition collapse in the face of Meredith Monk's vocalisations, and the way she works with her fellow musicians and performers. On one hand, hers is a virtuosity of 'extended vocal techniques', to borrow terminology from the musical avant-garde, but to babies who know how to cry and to Mongolian throat singers and Sami yoikkers, there is nothing unusual about the sounds she makes.

Apart from the occasional repeated phrase in English, like the 'mountains' and 'cities' and 'steam ships' and 'cinnabar' that Alexandra dreams of discovering at the start of the first part of the opera, the majority of the two hours and more of the music for *Atlas* contains no words. Instead, Monk and her performers sing syllables that refer to archetypal vowel and consonant sounds, over the earthy repetitions of her instrumental writing. Their meaning isn't contained by syntax, it's released instead by this non-semantic vocal transcendence.

That could be another excuse for avant-garde hermeticism, but the effect is just the opposite. There is nothing inscrutable about Meredith Monk's music in *Atlas*, or in any of the songs and theatre pieces and unclassifiable performances of her career. In fact, there's a naivety and a disarming directness about her musical storytelling. The Hungry Ghost is a terrifying apparition of musicalised shrieks and wails; those Ice Demons make an unmistakably glittering polyphony, to an accompaniment of the glass harmonica, an instrument of frosty uncanniness, wine glasses ringing into a chilly infinite.

Atlas's storytelling is clear, rigorous and absolute: it's a kind of musical communication that transgresses all the categories and separations of musical cultures only to connect them together in an utterly new way. Or rather, in a spectacularly primordial way, which any human audience anywhere could understand. Monk's non-linguistic vocalisations are more specific in their dramatic and expressive power than any sung language, but they are more global, too, in how they connect with features of our whole humanity, not its fractured parts.

For all its images of specific locations, its scenes of forests and campfires and airports and 'agricultural community', *Atlas* at the end describes an 'inner journey', as Alexandra closes her opera by returning to her first memory: the smell of that cup of coffee. The invitation of Meredith Monk's musical journey is similarly intimate, and similarly transformative: to have the certain knowledge of our innate connectedness as a human species across cultures, because every one of our voices is capable of meeting each other's on that plane of sound-making and vocal realisation that Monk has revealed to the world. There's a deep connection through time as well, because you feel, through the 'conduit', as she puts it, of her voice, as if you fall backwards through the aeons, to the places where the first sounds of love, and fear, and joy, and connection were made by our ancestors.

Meredith Monk and her music are living palimpsests that carry our deep species memory through her vocal music. Listen to her voice, and listen to the sounds of deep time collapsing into the urgency and wonder of today, of this moment, of this place – of her voice, and of yours. Enjoy the journey – and, just like Alexandra's epiphany at the end of *Atlas*, enjoy that cup of coffee.

PIECE #47

THOMAS ADÈS (1971–)

AMERICA –
A PROPHECY

New York, 1999

It was written as a 'Message for the Millennium', and first performed in New York in the embers of the previous aeon, in November 1999. Thomas Adès's *America – A Prophecy* borrows its title from William Blake's fantastical early nineteenth-century history on the foundation of the American Revolution to chart a much more direct, much darker, and much more genuinely prophetic vision of the beginnings and ends of cycles of human history: specifically, the cataclysms of the end of the Mayan Empire after the conquest of South America in the sixteenth century and beyond – and the collapse, in turn, of the empire that the conquistadores began and whose imperium still survives in today's America.

Written by a British composer then in his late twenties, *America – A Prophecy* claimed a historical overview that was ambitious and awe-inspiring, and in the substance of its music for orchestra, choir and mezzo-soprano soloist, it realised the sounds of the coming apocalypse, announced by the words the mezzo-soprano sings in the first part of the piece: 'Oh my nation / Prepare / The people move as in dreams / They are weak from fuck and drink ... It is the end of all our ways'.

America, 1999: Adès's inspirations for the piece and for this moment of the turning of the tide of time were to look back into America's deep past to find visions of its future. One of those epiphanies came in the forests of Belize, when he saw the

Mayan temples covered by the rainforest and had a vision of a far future in which Manhattan's skyscrapers would similarly be reclaimed by nature. The inevitability of the fall and rise of civilisations was something that the Mayans themselves foresaw. Adès knew the texts and poems of the *Chilam Balam*, which he had been reading on his first visit to the United States of America a few years before writing *America*, a collection called *The Destruction of the Jaguar*. 'Their prophecies of cyclic creation and destruction spoke to me so urgently'. His task in *America – A Prophecy* was to 'unlock their connection to our present and future as the millennium turned.'

Right from the start, the music is staged as a swirl of different kinds of time: repeated, urgent figures in the woodwind that speak of flight, anxiety, and a nervous present tense. But that frenetic energy is set within an abyss of deeper, slower time that the rest of the orchestra creates: music that glitters and falls and drips in the piano and percussion, and which looms ominously out of the depths. There's a clearing in the texture – like a moment when you look up and see a Mayan temple, or the Chrysler Building, enveloped by the forest – before we hear the mezzo-soprano declaiming her words. She is a Mayan prophet, singing from the summit of the temple, and seeing clearly her people's destiny. She sings as if consumed by a fever, faster and faster: 'They will come from the east / Their god stands on the pole / They will burn all the land / They will burn all the sky … Oh my nation'. And her terrifying prophecy is realised in the conquest of the chorus who suddenly enter with a blaze of trumpets and drums and bellicose terror, singing in Spanish: 'All the good soldiers who enlist in this war … will have in Heaven eternal glory'. That's set to music that Adès remakes from a sixteenth-century Spanish piece, 'La Guerra' by Mateo Flecha, music composed at the time of the conquistadores. Adès puts Flecha's piece through another dizzying wheel of musical time, amplifying its call to arms into a tableau of lurid – and thrilling – horror, scorching the earth and leaving the mezzo-soprano to mourn: 'They will rule from the backs of your fallen. It is foretold'.

This wasn't a message of hope for the millennium, as the commissioners, the New York Philharmonic, might have wanted for its audiences, but a searing revelation of a deep truth: that America's civilisation, along with every empire in human history, will surely fall, and will surely be replaced, as the Romans were, as the Mayans were. Adès transmutes that idea into endless cycles of musical time, layered on top of and next to one another. His music embodies that spiralling, that cycle of beginnings and ends, and he throws his listeners into the centre of that maelstrom so that we physically feel that process in action.

The second movement – the final part of the first version of this piece – is the chilling aftermath of conquest, as the mezzo sings 'we shall turn to ash' before a blasted climax in the orchestra, a slow scream that builds towards her final line: 'know this well / Ash feels no pain'. The chorus mutter a Latin text in which their conquest is shown to be sham and hubris: 'This is our victory / by which our faith conquers the world'. But there's no heroism in Adès's setting of these words: the chorus have turned into ghosts of the conquistadores' own civilisation crumbling to ruin.

And that is where the piece finished at its premiere in 1999, and in every other performance until very recently. But in

America after 9/11, this was a piece that US audiences were hardly ever exposed to, because programmers felt that its message of threats coming from the east and burning the sky were too literally prophetic of the attacks on the Twin Towers. The fact that, as a consequence, America and its allies visited the same civilisation-changing violence upon other countries only proved the piece's point the more clearly, sowing the seeds for the cycles of decay and rebirth to speed up, not to slow down.

But *America* the piece, and the prophecy, was not finished. In 2024, Adès wrote another, third movement because he said that it needed something to answer this 'stark, truncated ending'. Instead of this original 'cliff-drop, with no redemption', as he put it, in the new third movement, the chorus become the vanquished Mayans – and the vanquished of any empire.

Singing more words from the *Chilam Balam* texts, this movement makes the message of *America* clear: 'in every birth a death / In every death a birth … In every form a ruin / In every ruin a form / The wheel of time counts off the days, the years, the aeons'. As the mezzo-soprano joins the chorus, their roles are no longer that of a prophet and the conquistadores. They are all emissaries who sing from that 'twilight between nothing and being'. It's as if all the singers are flung out into the cosmos, surveying the cycles of those aeons from a gigantically zoomed-out viewpoint. It is a pitiless place, in which musical time is stretched out so that it becomes a slow hymn. The chorus sing with one voice, certain in their observation that 'this is the story of the world / the way it was / the way it shall be'. This knowledge is both chilling – cold, like the heat-death of the universe – and the proper resolution to *America*'s musical and existential trajectory, as the singers finally write another page in the 'book of years / The eternal turning towards our end'.

In daring to bring *America – A Prophecy* to this desolate and irresistible resolution, the piece holds up a mirror to our time, turning the truth that the gyres of history lead only to those spiralling places of empires rising and falling into physical, musical experience. It's a piece that fulfils its own prophecy. *America* is a vindication of its premonitory musical and poetic power, and it's a warning from the future: a message for this millennium and all the millennia to come.

PIECE #48

UNSUK CHIN (1961–)

ŠU, CONCERTO FOR SHENG AND ORCHESTRA

Tokyo, 2009

The question has always been, why has classical music clung to the myth of its separation from other musical cultures, in the very decades where the openness to influences from every part of the world has been a fact of our daily lives, in our trade, our geopolitics – and our culture? Not only that, why has one particular strand of Western music, the post-1945 avant-garde, made a deeper silo within a silo? In its attempt to vindicate the idea of its progressiveness and its break with the contaminated past, musical modernists have sometimes tried to show that musical value is all about hermetic, self-contained systems. That's opposed to the essence of the musical experience for the vast majority of listeners and audiences, its connection, and its communication with individuals, cultures and histories.

Unsuk Chin's music is vivid proof that all of the above are myths of classical and avant-garde protectionism, Europe-first ideologies that today's musical world will never stop disproving and joyfully shattering. Those myths are precisely that – untruths that hide a story of increasingly global interconnectedness that defines the sounds and substance of these repertoires.

And yet as a South Korean composer and musician studying in Germany in the 1980s, Unsuk Chin had to face a long journey to discover her own voice from the myriad influences and ideas that shaped her: the piano she was obsessed by growing up in Seoul, the energy and radical single-mindedness of the modernist traditions she was flung into in Germany, and the electronic experiments that showed her how the inside of sounds could contain so many musical multitudes.

It took her years of compositional silence before she launched a series of solo and ensemble pieces that revealed the depth and refinement of what she discovered, but it took decades longer than that for her to do something for the first time in her music, and to do so more successfully than any other composer has done: to write a concerto for a Western orchestra with a South-East Asian instrument, the sheng, as a soloist, while, in her own words, avoiding the 'danger of slipping into mere exoticism at all costs'.

Generations of Western composers before and after her have not only fallen into that trap, but have deliberately used the sounds and images of other cultures – especially those of the East – for cheap imitation and instant colouristic effect. That's true across composers and genres from Rimsky-Korsakov in the late nineteenth century to digital sampling libraries in today's world, in which the sounds of traditional instruments are available instantly to conjure the sounds of exotic lands, from Irish pipes to Japanese flutes, all without leaving your armchair and your sequencing software, without thinking about what these sounds mean, who played them and why. As a South Korean composer, Chin has known more worlds of sound from the traditional cultures of her homeland than any Western-trained musician, an experience that's only given her more sensitivity to honour and understand those traditions when she uses them.

In her concerto for sheng and orchestra, *Šu* (the title comes from Egyptian mythology, meaning 'air'), the world hears what's possible when all of those dangers are not only avoided, but in which the power dynamic of Western musical institutions' relationship with other cultures is turned on its head. The sheng is the Chinese mouth organ, the origins of which go back around 3,000 years. It has a South Korean cousin, the saenghwang, which is the instrument Chin has known since her childhood.

The sheng is a mouth-blown free-reed harmonica – to give the instrument its organological definition – and it makes sounds of unique richness. It's capable of ethereal yet sharp-edged sonic complexity. Like the harmonica, the instrument produces sound on the player's in- and out-breath, so it creates a miraculous musical continuity (unlike the majority of wind instruments, which work only by the musician's breathing out). In the higher notes that the sheng makes, the effect can be hypnotic and entrancing. It's like listening to a glittering circle of sound, as if you could hear what an angel's halo sounded like.

… which is exactly the kind of Westernised exoticism of language that Unsuk Chin resists in how she thinks of the sheng and how she composes for it. In her hands, and in the hands of the sheng star Wu Wei, for whom she wrote the concerto, the sheng isn't an ornament to gild the sonic panoply of the orchestra, but the means to rethink the entire soundworld of orchestral possibility. *Šu* begins with the sheng playing on its own, with characteristic arcs of breath making slow chordal music that sounds like the turning of harmonic crystals in the air. This is the distinctive soundworld that expands and takes over the orchestra. As Unsuk Chin says, the sheng can sound like and melt into every department of the orchestra – the strings, the brass, the woodwind, even the percussion section – and as the piece develops, it's as if the whole orchestra had become a gigantic sheng, exploring and excavating its unique worlds of sound.

That means discovering places of enormous friction and explosive violence as well as shimmering splendour. Unsuk Chin's isn't an exoticised vision of this meeting of an Eastern traditional instrument with the Western institution of the orchestra, and neither is it one in which the differences between them are ironed out into blancmangey, homogeneity. Chin is driven in this piece, as she is in all her other concertos for piano, cello, and violin, to create tension, discourse, and dissonance. In *Šu* all of that energy is released by her understanding of the sounds and meaning of the sheng, so the narrative journey, towards sounds of frightening energy, to return to the eerie calm of the opening, is inspired directly by the in- and out-breaths of the sheng itself.

The story the piece tells is, in part, a refracted testimony of the sheng's millennia-long history across the dynasties of China and the kingdoms and empires of Japan and Korea. But the real story of *Šu* is how it turns the forms and conventions of Western ideas and institutions – the concerto, the orchestra – into radically different entities. Unsuk Chin turns the Western orchestra towards a new purpose. In her music, the orchestra isn't a place in which the musics of other cultures are flattened out by its sonic power and historic dominance of concert hall cultures. In *Šu*, the sounds and ideas of the sheng transform the orchestra's essential qualities. It isn't the sheng that's 'othered' by the orchestra, which would be the effect of the exoticism that Chin so successfully avoids. It's the orchestra that's the 'other' of the sheng.

Unsuk Chin's music is the sound of a global cultural consciousness in action. Attending deeply to the sounds and traditions that she grew up with, in her relationship with the sheng, the saenghwang, and their repertoires, she transforms, renews, and disturbs the received wisdoms of the orchestra. Not a fusion, not an exotic trip, but a deep reorientation of the purpose of orchestral music to make new, meaningful and moving sounds from the place where cultures meet – and listen to one another.

PIECE #49

JOHN LUTHER ADAMS (1953–)

BECOME OCEAN

Seattle, 2013

What if music weren't just a representation, a picture, a dramatisation of ecology and our relationship to our environment, but an ecological phenomenon in its own right? At its root, this is true of all the music in this book: each of these pieces becomes its own physical experience of vibrations and musical viscera that our bodies feel whenever they're performed, whenever we listen to them. Music is profoundly metaphorical, since it can always stand for and relate to the ideas, stories, and histories that all of these pieces are connected to. But music is also the least metaphorical of all the arts, because it's a set of physical experiences that exist in time, a life-force of frequencies that we don't just listen to, but which we experience resonating through us, which are born in their beginnings and which expire at their ending.

For the American composer John Luther Adams, that's the fundamental musical and ecological truth that motivates his entire creative life. Living in the extreme wildernesses of Alaska and now inhabiting the desert of New Mexico, he has devoted his life to making music in and of the landscapes he knows so well. *Inuksuit* is a piece for percussionists who move through an outdoor space, turning any performance into a ritual with and for the landscape in which it's performed. Many of his other pieces take in the inspiration of birdsong, of the sounds of the forest, snowscapes, the tundra, and the desert.

In John Luther Adams's work, the goal isn't to write music about these natural phenomena, but to compose experiences in parallel with them, so that the composition, the performance, and our listening, are folded in to the natural wonders that inspired them. John Luther Adams answers the challenges of the Anthropocene age not by throwing his hands up in despair at the changing environment, but by inviting us to journey with him to a place where the truth of our interconnectedness with the natural world is turned into a revelation. That's an epiphany that music can embody with unique power, showing us our responsibilities to nature, and to each other. Music is a natural phenomenon. And so are we, as a species, and as musical communities.

In 2013, John Luther Adams's *Become Ocean* took these principles to new extremes of musical immersion. It's a 40-minute piece for orchestra that takes its title as the catalyst to turn the orchestra into an ocean of sound, and to overwhelm its listeners in waves of sound that denature the conventions of orchestral sonority in order to come closer to the awesome and frightening sublimity of the sea. To listen to *Become Ocean* is to become aware of our tiny human lives in the face of the ceaseless power of the currents of our seas, their ability to incubate our lives as a species, and the certainty that they can extinguish them too.

The title is borrowed, John Luther Adams says, from a poem by the American composer John Cage. Cage was writing about Lou Harrison's music, saying that 'listening to it we become ocean'. In his programme note for the piece, John Luther Adams interprets this idea not only to think about depths of musical sonority, but deep time, back and forward in the

Earth's history: 'Life on this earth first emerged from the sea. And as the polar ice melts and sea level rises, we humans find ourselves facing the prospect that once again we may quite literally become ocean.'

But this music doesn't do anything as obvious as scream or protest against climate change. Instead, it gives us what the writer Alex Ross has said 'may be the loveliest apocalypse in musical history'. It's a gorgeous maelstrom of waves of sound that emerge from the depths to take over the whole soundworld, a tessellating turbulence of interweaving patterns that mimics both the surface complexity of the ocean and its deepest currents. The effect is just as mesmerising and as vertiginous as those moments when you look out over the sea, and you realise that there's a point where your vision loses its bearings, in which distances collapse into the immediacy of the waves in front of you and expand towards the distant horizon. In the same way, your listening, your perception literally becomes part of the ocean of this piece, as you surf the waves upon soundwaves that John Luther Adams creates.

Yet 'apocalypse' is too human a term for the effect of *Become Ocean*. John Luther Adams makes a music that moves according to laws of musical nature that aren't about satisfying our human expectations of how a piece should move through time or the stories it should tell. This music's cresting of waves of density in its 40 minutes, sometimes building up slowly, sometimes erupting like a sudden tsunami, moves according to a logic that is out of reach of your understanding. The only choice is to submit to its power, and to stay afloat on its currents while you can.

Any performance of *Become Ocean* has its beginning and its end in the concert hall, but the piece seems to release forces that are never truly extinguished, that are still churning and teeming even when the sound stops. These are currents of energy that are unconcerned about the spans of our human lives and our destinies: we are of the ocean, and we will become ocean, and this music is the sound of that inevitability in action.

The expressive marking to the performers at the start of the score says that this music should be played as if it were 'inexorable'. The power of John Luther Adams's piece is that it demands our surrender to its forces of musical nature. And after any listening journey with this music, it's an experience you have to recover from – and react to. Luther Adams inspires an ecological awareness through the intensity of that musical engagement, through music becoming truly oceanic in its power, resonance, and significance. This is how to make audiences wake up to what's happening in the world in the ugly apocalypses of the climate crisis. *Become Ocean* is both a gorgeous underworld of sound, and a revelatory call to action.

PIECE #50

KAIJA SAARIAHO (1952–2023)

INNOCENCE

Aix-en-Provence, 2021

In the end, it's a question of responsibility: our lives today are lived in webs of consequences, in which the lines that separate our witnessing an action from our culpability in it are increasingly blurred; in which what used to be absolutes and certainties about truths and falsehoods, about who is in the right and who is in the wrong, have melted into ambiguities.

The Finnish composer Kaija Saariaho's last opera, *Innocence*, is a mirror to that chain of responsibility in which our lives in the twenty-first century are enmeshed. The title is profoundly and darkly ironic. She dares to put on stage the aftermath and the reality of a school shooting, in which 10 students and one teacher have been killed at an international school in Helsinki. That means making theatre out of what might seem like an impossible subject, but Saariaho's point isn't to write music for the perpetrator or to underscore the crime itself – he is never seen or heard in the opera – but to focus on the stories of the victims, and the ongoing trauma of guilt that the family of the shooter cannot escape.

We witness the students cowering in the school as the tragedy unfolds, and in the opera's second timeline 10 years later, we're at the wedding of the younger brother of the murderer. A waitress at the wedding reception is the mother of Markéta, one of the victims. She realises whose wedding it is, and she confronts the family, who reveal their secret to the bride, who has never been told about the murders. The brother cannot live with himself, with the knowledge that he and the killer used to practice shooting together. But he isn't the only one who is culpable. The schoolchildren who bullied him, his parents who didn't understand him, the school that could not stop him: every character on stage is implicated in the chain of events that leads to the shooting. *Innocence* shows that no one is truly innocent.

And it's how Saariaho sets these narratives in her music that counts, especially her vocal writing, setting a multi-lingual text by Sofe Aksanen and Aleksi Barrière. Saariaho casts her musical net incredibly wide, as broad as the polyglot languages and characters demand. There are nine languages we hear – Finnish, German, English, Czech, Romanian, Swedish, French, Spanish and Greek – reflecting the international school where the shooting is set, but also hinting at the many different types of vocal style that Saariaho uses. *Innocence* is an opera that has parts for actors who speak, for others who sing, for Finnish folk singers, as well as for conventionally operatic voices. That could create a babel of techniques in how the opera communicates, but it's a dramatic and a musical device that amplifies the individuality of each character, and which allows them to tell their own story. Saariaho answers the essential question that motivates any opera: why are these people singing? – by using the whole gamut of human vocal production, so that characters speak because they have to, sing because they must, and inhabit otherworldly vocal traditions because that's what their character needs.

That's most moving in Markéta's music: she appears as a pupil during the shooting; she is one of the victims, and is the ghostly daughter of the waitress at the wedding. Written for the Finnish folk singer Vilma Jää, Markéta's music includes the yelps and shouts and calls of Finnish traditional singing to make her a unique character in any large-scale opera. Markéta – or rather, her ghost – has the last lines in the opera: 'Mami, Mami, let me go.'

But the resonances that Saariaho's music casts cannot be let go. She finds a realm of dazzling darkness throughout the score, from its very opening sounds, a glittery ooze that envelops the audience, and which allows her to slip seamlessly between the two timelines of the opera.

Telling these stories, which other composers would not and could not dare to, was essential to Saariaho's life as a composer. She put narratives on stage from women's perspectives in history and in fiction that the canons of operatic history had never done before. In her second opera, *Adriana Mater*, the central character is the victim of rape in war-time. The opera is about her relationship with her son, as she wonders if he will grow up to be as violent as his father. In *Émilie*, Saariaho tells the story of Émilie du Châtelet, the eighteenth-century French intellectual who introduced the ideas of Isaac Newton to France, as a 75-minute monodrama, composed for the Finnish soprano Karita Mattila. Earlier in her life, Saariaho used to say that it mattered as much to her that she was a woman composer as the fact that she was left-handed. But in her later decades, she consciously turned her operatic story-telling towards female voices and stories, narratives that she felt operatic history and musical and political institutions had silenced, and which they still silence.

In opening up her opera to so many types of voices, Saariaho offers the art form a new way of engaging with the world, inviting a huge range of singers and performers to be part of the operatic experience. That's new for twenty-first-century opera, but it returns the art form to the principles of multimedia and contemporary urgency that it started with, all those centuries ago in Italy before 1600.

Innocence builds on that moral and creative courage. It was written at a time when Saariaho's illness was becoming more severe, and she knew that in what would be her last opera, she would hold a mirror to the whole of society: musical, cultural and political. *Innocence* is a call to the twenty-first-century world to reject the passivity of the way that stories are spoon-fed to us in the media. *Innocence* demands instead that we stain ourselves with the experience not only of witnessing an event like its school shooting, but also that we take our position and accept our own responsibility as viewers. Are we complicit? Are we part of the problem in the way we blithely consume the stories of the next school shooting, or any other comparable tragedy, in our media, in our socials? It's not only the actors and singers on stage: are we innocent?

After its nearly two hours of music, you are not the same as a listener. Or you shouldn't be. Demanding our attention, refusing to stand on the sidelines, being part of how the most tragic and essential stories of our time are told, *Innocence* says to us all: if you listen, you're involved. And if you're involved, you've got to take a stand, to be part of how these stories unfold, and to claim a place in how the history of our future will be shaped. Listen – and act.

EPILOGUE

Whenever you listen to these pieces, play them, or think about them, you're the latest link in the chain of a community of music-makers that goes back to the first time the piece was heard, performed and composed. That's the unique embodied knowledge that musical culture gives all of its participants: these are pieces that do not only belong to their creators; their meaning is only realised in the infinite interpretations that musicians and audiences give them, and continue to make for them.

You make that living history whenever and however you participate in them, whether you're listening on your commute, singing at home or performing at your local concert venue. They are all folded into the time and place of their creation, as this book has tried to show – but as I've also suggested, the beautiful democracy of how these musical cultures work means that they are made in a present tense that never ends: the now of performance, the now of listening, the now of your time, your place, your culture. Alone among the arts, music has that empathetic power to make us feel what the first musicians who sang and played these pieces felt, to connect viscerally with them, and also to make these pieces our own in every second of our engagement with them.

There's another quality that these pieces reveal: prophecy. It's not only Thomas Adès's piece. I believe that all of the pieces of music in this book, and millions like them, have a potentially prophetic power. That's because in their performances to come, these pieces will shape how the future sounds. They will mean different things, they will be played via technology and in contexts that we can't wholly imagine, but when they are performed and listened to and attended to, they will be part of future musical communities who will make them their own just as we make them part of our lives. Like every piece of music that's performable with a similar freedom and agency, these pieces aren't only the sounds of our past – they are the sounds of our future.

And underneath them all, the rotation of the Earth is still resonating through us, even when we can't directly hear it. In billions of years' time, that Earth-song itself will cease, as the planet is atomised into the even older and stranger song of the universe, those uncountable infinities of vibration that make everything from gravity waves to neutrinos to supernovas.

There is a long time – trillions and trillions of years – before that song is sung too, at the end of this era of the universe. So for the aeon of your lifetime, keep listening, exploring and celebrating what it means to be human, through the magical, time-travelling empathy machines of pieces of music – these 50, and the billions more out there in the world. Ours is a world that's singing, and dancing, and musicking, as our atoms do, as our species does, as our cultures and societies do. You're indivisibly a part of the biggest piece and the grandest performance of them all, which you're responsible for and which you're contributing to, every second of your lives: the piece of music called the history of our world. What does the next page of that story, of your story, sound like?

This BBC Radio 3 book was inspired by the discovery and imagination that Radio 3 gave me as a young listener in Glasgow in the 1980s. I couldn't believe it then – and it's still a miracle now – that Radio 3 gives immediate access to everyone to a millennium and more of the most life-changing music, in live performances and recordings from all over the world, and puts this music in the context of composers' lives and times. Radio 3 is living proof of how listening to this music matters, and how it can transform lives and open doors of imagination.

I've been broadcasting on Radio 3 since 2000, presenting *Music Matters* and Radio 3's contemporary music and Proms coverage for more than two decades, and *The Listening Service* from 2016–2024, in 250 editions that are all available on BBC Sounds. I now present Radio 3's Saturday Morning show. Whenever and however you tune into Radio 3, I guarantee your life just might be changed as mine was – and continues to be – by the range of music, insight, and imagination of what Radio 3 broadcasts, 24 hours a day.

ACKNOWLEDGEMENTS

This book couldn't have happened without Shammah Banerjee's patience and expert counsel at BBC Books, and neither would it have reached fruition without the inspiration of Albert DePetrillo, Katie Fisher and the whole team. My agent Stephen M. Morrison at Susanna Lea Associates was the guide and catalyst to spark the project into life. And the book would have been no more than a writer and broadcaster's pipe dream without Sam Jackson, Jeremy Evans and Edward Blakeman at Radio 3 and their invitation to create this compendium. They, and many others, have brought this book into being - above all, V and M-G, without whom nothing is possible, and for whom it's all done, always.

SOURCES FOR QUOTATIONS

Prologue
Graeme Lawson, *Sound Tracks: Uncovering Our Musical Past* (Bodley Head, 2024), p. 346.

Piece #1
Translations of Enheduanna from:
Black, J., et al, 'Inana and Ebih', *The Literature of Ancient Sumer* (Oxford University Press, 2006).

Betty De Shong Meador, *Princess, Priestess, Poet: The Sumerian Temple Hymns of Enheduanna* (University of Texas Press, 2009), pp. 20, 238.

Exaltation of Inanna translation from:
https://www.themorgan.org/sites/default/files/pdf/education/Exaltation-of-Inanna-by-Enheduanna.pdf

Quotation from the lamentation prayer:
Samuel Noah Kramer, 'The Weeping Goddess: Sumerian Prototypes of the Mater Dolorosa', *The Biblical Archaeologist* 46:2 (Spring 1983), p. 46.

Piece #2
Wilfrid Perrett, 'The Heritage of Greece in Music', *Proceedings of the Musical Association* (58th Session, 1931–1932), p. 85.

Armand D'Angour and Tom Phillips, eds., *Music, Text, and Culture in Ancient Greece* (Oxford University Press, 2018).

Piece #5
Fiona Maddocks, *Hildegard of Bingen: The Woman of her Age* (Faber and Faber, 2013).
Honey Meconi, *Hildegard of Bingen* (University of Illinois Press, 2018).

Piece #13
Quotation from Casulana at:
Laurie Stras, 'Newly Restored Madrigals by Maddalena Casulana'
https://www.womensongforum.org/2024/05/15/newly-restored-madrigals-by-maddulena-casulana/

Fieri Consort, Laurie Stras, *The Excellence of Women: Casulana and Strozzi* (Fieri Records, 2024).

Piece #19
Quotations from Isabella Leonarda and the *vicario generale* of Novara from:
Candace Smith, liner notes for *Leonarda: A Portrait of Isabella Leonarda* (Brilliant Classics, 2022).

Piece #25
Quotation from Dr Delany in:
David Hunter, *The Lives of George Frideric Handel* (The Boydell Press, 2015, p. 142.

Piece #27
Quotation from Joseph II in:
William Mann, *The Operas of Mozart* (Cassell, 1977), p. 366.

Piece #28
Translation of Beethoven's words from:
Jan Swafford, *Beethoven: Anguish and Triumph* (Faber and Faber, 2014), p. 848.

Ibid., p. 856.

Piece #29
Quotations from the book that accompanies the world premiere recording of the piece:
Louise Bertin, *Fausto* (Palazzetto Bru Zane, 2024).

Piece #31
Quotation from Patty Hill in:
Lily Rothman, 'The Long History of the "Happy Birthday" Song - And Its Copyright', *Time*, July 29, 2015.

Piece #32
Igor Stravinsky and Robert Craft, *Expositions and Developments* (Faber and Faber, 1981), pp. 147-8.

Igor Stravinsky, *An Autobiography* (W. W. Norton 1962), p.31.

Piece #34
Quotation from Vaughan Williams in:
Ralph Vaughan Williams, Letter to Ursula Wood, 4th October 1938 (Letter No. VWL1378 at vaughanwilliamsfoundation.org).

Piece #35
Rian Milan, 'In The Jungle', *Rolling Stone* 14 May 2000.

Quotation from Linda family from:
Sam Cullman, dir., *ReMastered: The Lion's Share* (Netflix, 2019).

Piece #36
Vladimir Putin speech at:
http://en.kremlin.ru/events/president/news/69134

Elizabeth Wilson, *Shostakovich: A Life Remembered* (Faber and Faber, 2006), pp. 174, 185.

Piece #37
Ashley Jackson, liner notes for *Margaret Bonds: The Ballad of the Brown King & Selected Songs* (AVIE Records, 2019).

Piece #41

Pauline Oliveros, *Sonic Meditations* (IngramSpark, 2022).

Pauline Oliveros, *Deep Listening: A Composer's Sound Practice* (iUniverse, 2005).

Pauline Oliveros, programme note for *Bye Bye Butterfly,* http://sfsound. org/tape/oliveros.html.

Piece #42

Kate Molleson, *Sound Within Sound* (Faber and Faber, 2022), pp. 163–181.

Piece #43

Tom Mustill, *How to Speak Whale: A Voyage into the Future of Animal Communication* (William Collins, 2023), p. 23.

Piece #44

Julius Eastman quotes from:
Buffalo Evening News, 17 July 1976.

'Spoken Introduction To The Northwestern University Concert', on *Julius Eastman: Unjust Malaise* (New World Records, 2005).

Introduction to 'Julius Eastman Creative Associates Tour (Part 1) 1974 at https://vimeo.com/75197042?fl=pl&fe=ti

Piece #45

Steve Reich quotes from:
Interview between Steve Reich and Mina Miller at the Music of Remembrance concert, Illsley Ball Nordstrom Recital Hall, Seattle, 23 April 2001.

Richard Taruskin, *The Danger of Music – and Other Anti-Utopian Essays* (University of California Press, 2009), pp 101-2.

Piece #46

Meredith Monk, *The Soul's Messenger,* in *Meredith Monk: The Recordings* (ECM, 2022).

Piece #47

Quotations from Thomas Adès in:
Thomas May, programme note for *America - A Prophecy.*

Piece #48

Quotation from Unsuk Chin at:

Interview with Maggie S. Lorelli, 12 February 2025,
https://www.icma-info.com/icma-winner-unsuk-chin-energy-and-experimentation/

Piece #49

Alex Ross, 'Water Music', *The New Yorker* (8 July and 15 July 2013).

John Luther Adams, programme note for *Become Ocean*, at https://www.wisemusicclassical.com/work/57008/Become-Ocean--John-Luther-Adams/